FOUR SUFI CLASSICS

SALAMAN AND ABSAL
THE NICHE FOR LIGHTS
THE WAY OF THE SEEKER
THE ABODE OF SPRING

Introduction
by

IDRIES SHAH

THE OCTAGON PRESS
LONDON

ISBN 0 900860 69 3

**Published for The Sufi Trust by
The Octagon Press**

First impression in this Edition 1980
Second impression 1984
Third impression 1994

Printed in Great Britain by
Redwood Books, Trowbridge, Wiltshire

CONTENTS

INTRODUCTION

Ghazzali, Sanai and Jami, authors of the four Classics presented here, are among the very greatest names in the Sufi tradition. The dates of our three sages range from Ghazzali's birth in 1058 (just before the Norman Conquest of Britain) until Jami's death in the year when the 'Moors' were expelled from Spain and, as many British schoolchildren repeat 'Fourteen hundred and ninety-two — Columbus sailed the ocean blue'.

In terms of Western categorization, the four classics may be described as follows:

Ghazzali: *Niche for Lights*, mystico-religious study of the 'Light-Verse' in the Koran;

Sanai: *The Way of the Seeker*, poetic rendering of the Way of spiritual realization;

Jami: *The Abode of Spring*, book of counsel for the spiritual aspirant;

Salaman and Absal, allegory of the soul's experiences on earth.

The dates of the translations range from the famous Edward Fitzgerald's *Salaman*, published in 1856, to the talented David Pendlebury's rendering from *The Way of the Seeker*, completed in 1979. The most ancient Persian book on the Sufi Way, Hujwiri's *Revelation of the Veiled*, written over a thousand years ago, before any of the classics which we reproduce here, quotes the Sufi ancient Fushanji as saying: 'Today Sufism is a name without a reality — formerly it was a reality without a name!' When Fushanji spoke, there was already a vast accumulation of Sufic lore from the early Masters; but Rumi had not been born; nor Hafiz: let alone Saadi or ny of the putative founders of the great Dervish Orders oɪ the Qadiri, Suhrawardi, Chishti and Naqshbandi. The Reality of Sufism did, indeed, continue, but the writings and ɛ˙tions of the teachers who followed produced a corpus of material which for the majority of people, perhaps, obscured the origin and purpose of the Path: increasing the element which can very truly be described as a 'name without a reality'.

The classical books themselves became a sort of holy writ, and instead of people finding their way by means of direct instruction in a Sufi circle, more and more emphasis was placed upon the study of the literature. An 'intellectual' and a cultish kind of 'Sufi' became commonplace. Following a familiar sociological (and sometimes called religious, though surely not a spiritual) pattern, the words became more prized than the content, and the mechanical performance of rituals superseded understanding of the actions and consequently inhibited their originally desired effect. Interestingly enough, it is the very misuse of books in this way which stimulated the masters to write more and more books: works which corresponded to updated textbooks in contemporary terms. Rumi, for example, wrote the *Masnavi* because his disciples relied too heavily on Attar and Sanai, his predecessors, and in so doing were following a literary-emotional, not a spiritual path.

The instruments themselves became the barriers: and those who have studied classical works will note how carefully the doctrine of supersession of materials became emphasized by the teachers. This factor was, perhaps, not so carefully observed by many readers, for two quite obvious reasons. First, the literary tradition everywhere can seldom bear to regard any writings, especially those by revered figures, as obsolete. The very conception is anathema to the literary and historico-religious mind. Second, Sufis tended to teach in basic terms. They would not necessarily say: 'such-and-such a book is useless to us today', because they preferred to direct attention to the principle, not the example. Instead they taught and wrote: 'Attachment to the instrument, observing the container not the content, is a sign of worldliness ...' They also, as has more often been accepted, campaigned against arid scholasticism and pedantry.

Sufi books, then, are instrumental, not informational or for imparting secrets or pleasure. The Sufis said, as did Abu-Amr of Damascus, 'Sufism is to close the eyes to the created world', and, in the words of Ibn al-Jalla, 'Sufism is truth which has no form'. Sufis have to 'Be in the world but not of the world'. But, it has often been asked, how can something 'of the world', like a book or a person, be of any account if Sufism is of such a refined nature that it involves detachment from these things?

The answer lies in the dictum: 'The apparent is the bridge to the Real'. The fertilizer which you put on your crops may be something of no account, but it is, instrumentally speaking, vital. The fault lies in the worship of the fertilizer. The Sufi book is designed to help to provoke states in the aspirant where the book is no longer needed. The great Sufi sage Nuri referred to this when he said, 'Rather than forms of knowledge and practices, Sufism is characteristics'.

The would-be Sufi can learn from situations, from books, from people and above all from his teacher, only to the extent to which certain characteristics are abandoned and certain others nurtured. The importance of this 'posture induction' is stressed by Abu-Hafs ('the Blacksmith') of Nishapur, another ancient authority, in his words: 'Sufism is wholly behaviour. There is a form of behaviour for every time and for every place and every state. Whoever accords with the conduct of occasion reaches the attainment of realized man. But who neglects the requirements of behaviour is far from nearness (to Truth) . . . and excluded from acceptance'.

Hence Sufi literature (as, indeed, Sufi practices and theories) must be viewed from a standpoint which is unfamiliar to most people involved in religious and literary pursuits. The use of the materials approximates more closely to that employed by modern scientists: and, in fact, a large number of the historical Sufis were active in science. Many of them continue so today.

The would-be Sufi: To the majority of people in the West, and to a very large number who think that they know something about the subject in the East as well, a 'would-be Sufi' must be someone who has not yet started to call himself a Sufi, since he has not been initiated or otherwise involved in Sufi matters. This is because the term *Sufi* is generally taken to mean 'someone who believes in Sufism', or 'someone who has been accepted by someone else as a Sufi'. This deterioration of the real significance of the term in ordinary usage only under-lines that those who use it in this manner are not Sufis at all. Hujwiri, just quoted, stresses that, since there is no meaning for the term Sufi (as the experience is in-communicable, and you cannot say: 'I am a Sufi' and be understood by everyone, as you would say 'I am a Turk' and people know what that means) nobody may call himself a Sufi. This does not prevent thousands, perhaps millions, of people even in the present day, from describing themselves as Sufis. '*Sufi*', notes Hujwiri, (*Kashf*, Chapter on Sufism) 'is a name which is given to perfect saints and spiritual adepts . . . The perfect are called *Sufi* and the Seekers are called *Mutasawwif* [attempting to be a Sufi]'. There is a third class — and this is one to which almost all publicly-known 'Sufis' belong — and that is of those who attempt to make themselves like the Sufis. Hujwiri very succinctly categorizes the three types as The *Man of Union* (unified with the Ultimate Reality, God); the *Man of Principles* (whoever goes by rules and dogma, including those who merely try to be Sufis through attempts to make a system work) and the *Man of Superfluities* (people who are not harmonized with Truth and who do not follow patterns, but indulge themselves emotionally and with fantasy).

From this it will be seen that the ever-increasing number and variety of 'mystics' in the West especially, have their counterpart in the East where their limitations and characteristics have been well understood for centuries. It is hoped that a similar perception of the differences between the approaches will eventually develop in the West and among those influenced by it, though innocent of study of this clear tradition of assessment.

The classics presented here offer good examples of materials which have developmental content, but still have been treated as holy writ by some, as superior or inferior poetry by others, as materials for a study of the mentality of their authors by yet others. They form a useful body of material because their outward dissimilarity conceals an inner consonance. And that inwardness is not on the shallow level usually assumed. If you read commentaries on these pieces by a wide variety of writers, you will notice that the analysis seldom goes deeper than 'discovering' that the working hypothesis of all three Sufis is the same: that there is an ultimate Reality, absolute Truth, referred to as God, and that human beings can contact this by certain methods known to the people of this Tradition. But the underlying patterns, once the layers of subjectivity are stripped off and the personal aspirations and assumptions removed, are of abiding value.

Both the translations and the comments of these four works serve to illustrate rather neatly the preoccupations of the scholars and others who have presented them, and the current interests of the age in which they are centred. This extra dimension, which might make the translations tiresome and outdated to an ordinary contemporary reader, serves the Sufi contention well: people look for what they want to find, and fail to find what they do not want. Equally, cultural and local style as well as scholarly knowledge and ability strongly mark much academic work, and have to be allowed for.

Of the three translators, I would say that Fitzgerald exposes his preoccupations well enough, in his prefatory Letter to Professor Cowell, and Pendlebury has not allowed personal biases to intrude into the text. But Canon Gairdner (1873–1928) is worth looking at as an example of how someone may achieve a tolerable translation of an Arabic document and yet fail to understand it; to the extent that he almost querulously lists points which baffle him, in his Introduction to *The Niche*.

It has often been observed by Sufis (and later by

modern psychologists) that emotion can so blunt the understanding of even the best scholar that he will perform at a level perplexingly low and embarrassingly trite. Hence, for instance, there is no problem for anyone who had read the materials on Sufism available during Gairdner's time to discern as to why Ghazzali listed some 'reputable Moslems' together with idolators and dualists. All Sufis and many of their readers know that the Sufis may call anyone an idolator who is fixated on secondary things, and dualists are people who (whether overtly or otherwise) adopt a dualistic mentality. Their repute as Moslems or anything else does not prevent their diagnosis as 'idolators or dualists'. The same line of interpretation will almost immediately solve all the other perplexities which so confused poor Gairdner.

Gairdner, it is true, does not seem to claim much knowledge of Sufism. He says himself that he first saw and talked to some Sufis, in Potsdam, in 1910, and did not understand them. The following year he first saw the *Niche*, and he translated it the same year. Further evidence of his continuing lack of knowledge about the Sufis might be found in his choice of a dervishes' cave in 1914, while a Christian missionary in Cairo, as a place in which to invoke the help of the devil in a supernatural murder which he attempted to bring about. But perhaps in fairness to him we should give the story as we find it in the very reverential biography published by the Society for Promoting Christian Knowledge*.

Temple Gairdner ('of Cairo') worked for just under thirty years as a missionary in Egypt. He was horrified when, about Easter 1914, he found that one of his flock had become a Moslem and was recruiting others. He called members of his community together and took them to a dervish cave near the Pyramids. According to his friend Dr Harpur, this good man then proposed that a curse be put on the defector, and the name of the Devil

---

*C. E. Padwick, *Temple Gairdner of Cairo*, SPCK, London (2nd ed) 1930, p. 221.

invoked, so that his spirit be saved in the day of Jesus Christ. Perhaps not surprisingly, some did not want to do it, but the doctor continues that 'only one or two fell away'. His biographer asserts that the severity of Gairdner's speech was 'only the right of those who have gone to all lengths in love and prayer'.

If Canon Gairdner's speech and actions were to be regarded within the customary meaning of the words in which we find them, they can only mean that the Christianity of the Canon and even of his biographer, perhaps, and most of his flock, included the following interesting ideas:

1. Love and prayer can be exhausted, after which one is entitled to hate;

2. One form of such hate is to desire the death of another;

3. The majority of a Christian community may agree to invoking the Devil for the sake of the Church;

4. A major missionary and Canon, of 30 years' evangelical experience, may resort to a dervish cave near the Pyramids to curse and seek the death of a defector.

One is reminded of the Persian proverb:

Chun kufr az Ka'aba bar ayad — kuja manad Musulmani? (When infidelity rises from the Ka'aba [mosque of Mecca] — where can Islam remain?)

On this showing, Canon Gairdner knew very little about Christianity, and not much more about Sufism. It is very likely that this translation of his from Ghazzali, which is textually not at all bad, was prepared by some Egyptian for him, at least in large part.

There is a double advantage in looking at the mentality of the greatly-loved British missionary and his translation from the point of view of his extraordinary death-ritual. First, it enables us to treat his perplexities and comments with some reserve. Second, and perhaps more usefully, it strikingly parallels in eccentricity the behaviour of some of the cults and their consequences which have for centuries, perhaps from the earliest days, accompanied all religions and formed a part of their lunatic fringe. So, next time you are told that the Sufis are 'Mohammedan fanatics' or 'members of Islamic excitatory cults', just remember that the most reverend Canon Temple Gairdner would have been in more appropriate company if he had joined a company of Dancing or Howling Dervishes — those ridiculous deteriorations of an ancient and reputable Teaching — than if he had found himself among real Sufis or, for that matter, perhaps real Christians who, as we know, love their enemies.

Ghazzali, Sanai and Jami are all representatives of the authentic tradition.

I

SALAMAN AND ABSAL

LETTER TO PROFESSOR COWELL

My dear Cowell,

Two years ago, when we began (I for the first time) to read this Poem together, I wanted you to translate it, as something that should interest a few who are worth interesting. You, however, did not see the way clear then, and had Aristotle pulling you by one Shoulder and Prakrit Vararuchi by the other, so as indeed to have hindered you up to this time completing a Version of Háfiz' best Odes which you had then happily begun. So, continuing to like old Jámí more and more, I must try my hand upon him; and here is my reduced Version of a small Original. What Scholarship it has is yours, my Master in Persian, and so much beside; who are no further answerable for *all* than by well liking and wishing publisht what you may scarce have Leisure to find due fault with.

Had all the Poem been like Parts, it would have been all translated, and in such Prose lines as you measure Háfiz in, and such as any one should adopt who does not feel himself so much of a Poet as him he translates and some he translates for — before whom it is best to lay the raw material as genuine as may be, to work up to their own better Fancies. But, unlike Háfiz' best – (whose Sonnets are sometimes as close packt as Shakespeare's, which they resemble in more ways than one) — Jámí, you know, like his Countrymen generally, is very diffuse in what he tells and his way of telling it. The very structure of the Persian Couplet — (here, like people on the Stage, I am repeating to you what you know, with an Eye

3

to the small Audience beyond) — so often ending with the same Word, or Two Words, if but the foregoing Syllable secure a lawful Rhyme, so often makes the Second Line but a slightly varied Repetition, or Modification of the First, and gets slowly over Ground often hardly worth gaining. This iteration is common indeed to the Hebrew Psalms and Proverbs — where, however, the Value of the Repetition is different. In your Háfiz also, not Two only, but Eight or Ten Lines perhaps are tied to the same Close of Two — or *Three* — words; a verbal Ingenuity as much valued in the East as better Thought. And how many of all the Odes called his, more and fewer in various Copies, do you yourself care to deal with? — And in the better ones how often some lines, as I think for this reason, unworthy of the Rest — interpolated perhaps from the Mouths of his many Devotees, Mystical and Sensual — or crept into Manuscripts of which he never arranged or corrected one from the First?

This, together with the confined Action of Persian Grammar, whose organic simplicity seems to me its difficulty when applied, makes the Line by Line Translation of a Poem not line by line precious tedious in proportion to its length. Especially — (what the Sonnet does not feel) — in the Narrative; which I found when once eased in its Collar, and yet missing somewhat of rhythmical Amble, somehow, and not without resistance on my part, swerved into that 'easy road' of Verse — easiest as unbeset with any exigencies of Rhyme. Those little Stories, too, which you thought untractable, but which have their Use as well as Humour by way of quaint Interlude Music between the little Acts, felt ill at ease in solemn Lowth-Isaiah Prose, and had learn'd their tune, you know, before even Hiawatha came to teach people to quarrel about it. Till, one part drawing on another, the Whole grew to the present form.

As for the much bodily omitted — it may be readily guessed that an Asiatic of the 15th Century might say much on such a subject that an Englishman of the 19th would not care to read. Not that our Jámí is ever *licentious* like his Contemporary Chaucer, nor like Chaucer's Posterity in Times that called themselves more Civil. But better Men will not now endure a simplicity of Speech that Worse men abuse. Then the many more, the foolisher, Stories — preliminary Te Deums to Allah and Allah's-shadow Sháh — very much about Alef Noses, Eyebrows like inverted Núns, drunken Narcissus Eyes — and that eternal Moon Face which never wanes from Persia — of all which there is surely enough in this Glimpse of the Original. No doubt some Oriental character escapes — the Story sometimes becomes too Skin and Bone without due interval of even Stupid and Bad. Of the two Evils? — At least what I have chosen is least in point of bulk; scarcely in proportion with the length of its Apology which, as usual, probably discharges one's own Conscience at too great a Price; people at once turning against you the Arms they might have wanted had you not laid them down. However it may be with this, I am sure a complete Translation — even in Prose — would not have been a readable one — which, after all, is a useful property of most Books, even of Poetry.

In studying the Original, you know, one gets contentedly carried over barren Ground in a new Land of Language — excited by chasing any new Game that will but show Sport; the most worthless to win asking perhaps all the sharper Energy to pursue, and so far yielding all the more Satisfaction when run down. Especially, cheered on as I was by such a Huntsman as poor Dog of a Persian Scholar never hunted with before; and moreover — but that was rather in the Spanish Sierras — by the Presence of a Lady in the Field, silently brightening about us like Aurora's Self, or chiming in with musical Encouragement that all we started and ran down must be Royal Game!

Ah, happy Days! When shall we Three meet again — when dip in that unreturning Tide of Time and Circumstance! — In those Meadows far from the World, it seemed, as Salámán's Island — before an Iron Railway broke the Heart of that Happy Valley whose Gossip was the Millwheel, and Visitors the Summer Airs that momentarily ruffled the sleepy Stream that turned it as they chased one another over to lose themselves in Whispers in the Copse beyond. Or returning — I suppose you remember whose Lines they are—

> When Winter Skies were tinged with Crimson still
> Where Thornbush nestles on the quiet hill,
> And the live Amber round the setting Sun,
> Lighting the Labourer home whose Work is done,
> Burn'd like a Golden Angel-ground above
> The solitary Home of Peace and Love—

at such an hour drawing home together for a fireside Night of it with Aeschylus or Calderon in the Cottage, whose walls, modest almost as those of the Poor who clustered — and with good reason — round, make to my Eyes the Towered Crown of Oxford hanging in the Horizon, and with all Honour won, but a dingy Vapour in Comparison. And now, should they beckon from the terrible Ganges, and this little Book begun as a happy Record of past, and pledge perhaps of future, Fellowship in Study, darken already with the shadow of everlasting Farewell!

But to turn from you Two to a Public — nearly as numerous — (with whom, by the way, this Letter may die without a name that *you* know very well how to supply) — here is the best I could make of Jámí's Poem — 'Ouvrage de peu d'étendue', says the Biographie Universelle, and, whatever that means, here collapsed into a nutshell Epic indeed; whose Story however, if nothing else, may interest some Scholars as one of Persian Mysticism — perhaps the grand Mystery of all Religions — an Allegory fairly devised and carried out — dramatically culminating as it goes on; and told as to this day the East loves to tell her Story, illustrated by Fables and Tales, so often (as we read in the latest Travels) at the expense of the poor Arab of the Desert.

The Proper Names — and some other Words peculiar

6

to the East — are printed as near as may be to their native shape and sound — 'Sulaymán' for Solomon — 'Yúsuf' for Joseph, &c., as being not only more musical, but retaining their Oriental flavour unalloyed with European Association. The *accented* Vowels are to be pronounced long, as in Italian — Salámán — Absál — Shírín, &c.

The Original is in rhymed Couplets of this measure—

which those who like Monkish Latin may remember in
    Dum Salámán verba Regis cogitat,
    Pectus intrá de profundis aestuat.
or in English — by way of asking, 'your Clemency for us and for our Tragedy'—
    Of Salámán and of Absál hear the Song;
    Little wants Man here below, nor little long
[1856]

NOTICE OF JÁMÍ'S LIFE

Drawn from Rosenzweig's 'Biographische Notizen' of the Poet.

NÚRUDDÍN ABDURRAHMAN, Son of Mauláná Nizámuddín Ahmed, and descended on the Mother's side from one of the Four great 'FATHERS' of Islam, was born A.H. 817, A.D. 1414, in Jám, a little Town of Khorásán, whither his Grandfather had removed from Desht of Ispahán and from which the poet ultimately took his Takhallus, or Poetic name, JÁMÍ. This word also signifies 'A Cup;' wherefore, he says, 'Born in Jám, and dipt in the '*Jám*' of Holy Lore, for a double reason I must be called JÁMÍ in the Book of Song'.[1] He was celebrated afterwards in other Oriental Titles — 'Lord of Poets' — 'Elephant of Wisdom', &c., but latterly liked to call himself 'The Ancient of Herát', where he mainly resided, and eventually died.

When Five Years old he received the name of Núruddín, the 'Light of Faith', and even so early began to show the Metal, and take the Stamp that distinguished him through Life. In 1419, a famous Sheikh, Khwájah Mohammed Pársá, then in the last Year of his Life, was being carried through Jám. 'I was not then Five Years old', says Jámí, 'and my Father, who with his Friends went forth to salute him, had me carried on the Shoulders of one of the Family and set down before the Litter of the Sheikh, who gave a Nosegay into my hand. Sixty Years have passed, and methinks I now see before me the bright Image of the Holy Man, and feel the Bless-

---

[1] He elsewhere plays upon his name, imploring God that he may be accepted as a Cup to pass about that Spiritual Wine of which the Persian Mystical Poets make so much.

ing of his Aspect, from which I date my after Devotion to that Brotherhood in which I hope to be enrolled'.

So again, when Mauláná Fakhruddín Loristání had alighted at his Mother's house — 'I was then so little that he set me upon his Knee, and with his Fingers drawing the Letters of "ALÍ" and "OMAR" in the Air, laughed with delight to hear me spell them. He also by his Goodness sowed in my Heart the Seed of his Devotion, which has grown to Increase within me — in which I hope to live, and in which to die. Oh God! Dervish let me live, and Dervish die; and in the Company of the Dervish do Thou quicken me to life again!'

Jámí first went to a School at Herát; and afterward to one founded by the Great Timúr at Samarcand. There he not only outstript his Fellow-students in the very Encyclopaedic Studies of Persian Education, but even puzzled his Doctors in Logic, Astronomy, and Theology; who, however, with unresenting Gravity welcomed him — 'Lo! a new Light added to our Galaxy!' — And among them in the wider Field of Samarcand he might have liked to remain, had not a Dream recalled him to Herát. A Vision of the Great Súfí Master there, Mohammed Saaduddin Káshgharí, appeared to him in his Sleep, and bade him return to One who would satisfy all Desire. Jámí returned to Herát; he saw the Sheikh discoursing with his Disciples by the Door of the Great Mosque; day after day passed him by without daring to present himself; but the Master's Eye was upon him; day by day drew him nearer and nearer — till at last the Sheikh announces to those about him — 'Lo! this day have I taken a Falcon in my Snare!'

Under him Jámí began his Súfí Noviciate, with such Devotion, both to Study and Master, that going, he tells us, but for one Summer Holiday into the Country, a single Line sufficed to 'lure the Tassel-gentle back again';

Lo! here am I, and Thou look'st on the Rose!

10

By-and-by he withdrew, by due course of Súfí Instruction, into Solitude so long and profound, that on his return to Men he had almost lost the Power of Converse with them. At last, when duly taught, and duly authorized to teach as Súfí Doctor, he yet would not take upon himself so to do, though solicited by those who had seen such a Vision of him as had drawn himself to Herát; and not till the Evening of his Life was he to be seen taking that place by the Mosque which his departed Master had been used to occupy before.

Meanwhile he had become Poet, which no doubt winged his Reputation and Doctrine far and wide through a People so susceptible of poetic impulse.

'A Thousand times', he says, 'I have repented of such Employment; but I could no more shirk it than one can shirk what the Pen of Fate has written on his Forehead' — 'As Poet I have resounded through the World; Heaven filled itself with my Song, and the Bride of Time adorned her Ears and Neck with the Pearls of my Verse, whose coming Caravan the Persian Háfiz and Saadí came forth gladly to salute, and the Indian Khosrau and Hasan hailed as a Wonder of the World'. 'The Kings of India and Rúm greet me by Letter: the Lords of Irák and Tabríz load me with Gifts; and what shall I say of those of Khorásán, who drown me in an Ocean of Munificence?'

This, though Oriental, is scarcely bombast. Jámí was honoured by Princes at home and abroad, at the very time they were cutting one another's Throats; by his own Sultan Abú Saïd; by Hasan Beg of Mesopotamia — 'Lord of Tabríz' — by whom Abú Saïd was defeated, dethroned, and slain; by Mohammed II. of Turkey — 'King of Rúm' — who in his turn defeated Hasan; and lastly by Husein Mírzá Baikará, who somehow made away with the Prince whom Hasan had set up in Abú Saïd's Place at Herát. Such is the House that Jack builds in Persia.

As Hasan Beg, however — the USUNCASSAN of old European Annals — is singularly connected with the

11

present Poem, and with probably the most important event in Jámí's Life, I will briefly follow the Steps that led to that as well as other Princely Intercourse.

In A.H. 877, A.D. 1472, Jámí set off on his Pilgrimage to Mecca, as every True Believer who could afford it was expected once in his Life to do. He, and, on his Account, the Caravan he went with, were honourably and safely escorted through the interjacent Countries by order of their several Potentates as far as Baghdád. There Jámí fell into trouble by the Treachery of a Follower whom he had reproved, and who misquoted his Verse into disparagement of ALÍ, the Darling Imám of Persia. This, getting wind at Baghdád, was there brought to solemn Tribunal. Jámí came victoriously off; his Accuser was pilloried with a dockt Beard in Baghdád Market-place: but the Poet was so ill pleased with the stupidity of those who have believed the Report, that, in an after Poem, he called for a Cup of Wine to seal up Lips of whose Utterance the Men of Baghdád were unworthy.

After four months' stay there, during which he visited at Helleh the Tomb of Alí's Son Husein, who had fallen at Kerbela, he set forth again — to Najaf, (where he says his Camel sprang forward at sight of Alí's own Tomb) — crossed the Desert in twenty-two days, continually meditating on the Prophet's Glory, to Medina; and so at last to MECCA, where, as he sang in a Ghazal, he went through all Mohammedan Ceremony with a Mystical Understanding of his Own.

He then turned Homeward: was entertained for forty-five days at Damascus, which he left the very Day before the Turkish Mohammed's Envoys came with 5000 Ducats to carry him to Constantinople. On arriving at Amida, the Capital of Mesopotamia, he found War broken out and in full Flame between that Sultan and Hasan Beg, King of the Country, who caused Jámí to be honourably escorted through the dangerous Roads to Tabríz; there received him in full Diván, and would fain have him abide at his Court awhile. Jámí, however, was intent on Home, and once more seeing his aged Mother

— for *he* was turned of Sixty — and at last reached Herát in the Month of Shaabán, 1473, after the Average Year's absence.

This is the HASAN, 'in Name and Nature *Handsome*' (and so described by some Venetian Ambassadors of the Time), who was Father of YAKÚB BEG, to whom Jámí dedicated the following Poem; and who, after the due murder of an Elder Brother, succeeded to the Throne; till all the Dynasties of 'Black and White Sheep' together were swept away a few years after by Ismaíl, Founder of the Sofí Dynasty in Persia.

Arrived at home, Jámí found Husein Mírzá Baikará, last of the Timuridæ, seated on the Throne there, and ready to receive him with open Arms. Nizámuddín Alí Shír, Husein's Vizír, a Poet too, had hailed in Verse the Poet's Advent from Damascus as 'The Moon rising in the West'; and they both continued affectionately to honour him as long as he lived.

Jámí sickened of his mortal Illness on the 13th of Moharrem, 1492 — a Sunday. His Pulse began to fail on the following Friday, about the Hour of Morning Prayer, and stopped at the very moment when the Muezzín began to call to Evening. He had lived Eighty-one Years. Sultan Husein undertook the pompous Burial of one whose Glory it was to have lived and died in Dervish Poverty; the Dignitaries of the Kingdom followed him to the Grave; where twenty days afterward was recited in presence of the Sultan and his Court an Eulogy composed by the Vizír, who also laid the first Stone of a Monument to his Friend's Memory — the first Stone of 'Tarbet'i Jámí', in the Street of Meshhed, a principal Thoro'fare of the City of Herát. For, says Rosenzweig, it must be kept in mind that Jámí was reverenced not only as a Poet and Philosopher, but as a Saint also; who not only might work a Miracle himself, but leave such a Power lingering about his Tomb. It was known that an Arab, who had falsely accused him of selling a Camel he knew to be unsound, died very shortly after, as Jámí had predicted, and on the very selfsame spot where the

Camel fell. And that libellous Rogue at Baghdád — he, putting his hand into his Horse's Nose-bag to see if the beast had finisht his Corn, had his Forefinger bitten off by the same — from which 'Verstümmlung' he soon died — I suppose, as he ought, of Lock-jaw.

The Persians, who are adepts at much elegant Ingenuity, are fond of commemorating Events by some analogous Word or Sentence whose Letters, cabalistically corresponding to certain Numbers, compose the Date required. In Jámí's case they have hit upon the word 'KÁS', A Cup, whose signification brings his own name to memory, and whose relative letters make up his 81 years. They have *Tárikhs* also for remembering the Year of his Death: Rosenzweig gives some; but Ouseley the prettiest of all;—

Dúd az Khorásán bar ámed—
'The smoke' of Sighs 'went up from Khorásán'.

No Biographer, says Rosenzweig cautiously, records of Jámí's having more than one Wife (Granddaughter of his Master Sheikh) and Four Sons; which, however, are Five too many for the Doctrine of this Poem. Of the Sons, Three died Infant; and the Fourth (born to him in very old Age), and for whom he wrote some Elementary Tracts, and the more famous 'Beháristán,' lived but a few years, and was remembered by his Father in the Preface to his Kiradnáma-i Iskander — Alexander's Wisdom-book — which perhaps had also been begun for the Boy's Instruction. He had likewise a nephew, one Mauláná Abdullah, who was ambitious of following his Uncle's Footsteps in Poetry. Jámí first dissuaded him; then, by way of trial whether he had a Talent as well as a Taste, bade him imitate Firdausi's Satire on Sháh Mahmúd. The Nephew did so well, that Jámí then encouraged him to proceed; himself wrote the first Couplet of his First (and most celebrated) Poem — Laila and Majnún—

This Book of which the Pen has now laid the Foundation. May the diploma of Acceptance one day befall it, —

and Abdullah went on to write that and four other Poems which Persia continues to delight in to the present day, remembering their Authors under his Takhallus of HÁTIFÍ — 'The Voice from Heaven' — and Last of the classic Poets of Persia.

Of Jámí's literary Offspring, Rosenzweig numbers forty-four. But Shír Khán Lúdí in his 'Memoirs of the Poets', says Ouseley, accounts him Author of *Ninety-nine* Volumes of Grammar, Poetry, and Theology, which, he says, 'continue to be universally admired in all parts of the Eastern World, Írán, Túrán, and Hindústán' — copied some of them into precious Manuscripts, illuminated with Gold and Painting, by the greatest Penmen and Artists of the time; one such — the 'Beháristán' — said to have cost some thousands of pounds — autographed as their own by two Sovereign Descendants of TIMÚR and now reposited away from 'the Drums and Tramplings' of Oriental Conquest in the tranquil seclusion of an English library.

With us, his Name is almost wholly associated with his 'Yúsuf and Zulaikhá'; the 'Beháristán' aforesaid: and this present 'Salámán and Absál', which he tells us is like to be the last product of his Old Age. And these three Poems count for three of the brother Stars of that Constellation into which his seven best Mystical Poems are clustered under the name of 'HEFT AURANG' — those 'SEVEN THRONES' to which we of the West and North give our characteristic name of 'Great Bear' and 'Charles's Wain'.

This particular Salámán Star, which thus conspicuously figures in Eastern eyes, but is reduced to one of very inferior magnitude as seen through this English Version — is one of many Allegories under which the Persian Mystic symbolized an esoteric doctrine which he dared not — and probably could not — more intelligibly reveal. As usual with such Poems in the story-loving East, the main Fable is intersected at every turn with some other subsidiary story, more or less illustrative of

the matter in hand: many of these of a comic and grotes-
que Character mimicking the more serious, as may the
Gracioso of the Spanish Drama. As for the metre of the
Poem, it is the same as that adopted by Attár, Jeláluddín
and other such Poets — and styled, as I have heard, the
'Metre Royal' — although not having been used by Firdausí for his Sháh-námeth. Thus it runs:

$$\_ \cup \_ \_ | \_ \cup \_ \_ | \_ \cup \_ |$$

a' pace which, to those not used to it, seems to bring one
up with too sudden a halt at the end of every line to
promise easy travelling through an Epic. It may be
represented in Monkish Latin Quantity:

> Dum Sálámán verba Regis cogitat,
> Pectus illi de profundis aestuat;

or by English accent in two lines that may also plead for
us and our Allegory:

> Of Sálámán and of Absál hear the Song;
> Little wants man here below, nor little long.

PRELIMINARY INVOCATION

OH Thou, whose Spirit through this universe,
In which Thou dost involve thyself diffused,
Shall so perchance irradiate human clay
That men, suddenly dazzled, lose themselves
In ecstasy before a mortal shrine
Whose Light is but a Shade of the Divine;
Not till thy Secret Beauty through the cheek
Of LAILA smite doth she inflame MAJNÚN;[1]
And not till Thou have kindled SHÍRÍN'S Eyes
The hearts of those two Rivals swell with blood.
For Loved and Lover are not but by Thee,
Nor Beauty; — mortal Beauty but the veil

---

[1] Well-known Types of Eastern Lovers. SHÍRÍN and her Suitors
figure on p. 39.

16

Thy Heavenly hides behind, and from itself
Feeds, and our hearts yearn after as a Bride
That glances past us veil'd — but ever so
That none the veil from what it hides may know.
How long wilt thou continue thus the World
To cozen[1] with the fantom of a veil
From which thou only peepest? I would be
Thy Lover, and thine only — I, mine eyes
Seal'd in the light of Thee to all but Thee,
Yea, in the revelation of Thyself
Lost to Myself, and all that Self is not
Within the Double world that is but One.
Thou lurkest under all the forms of Thought,
Under the form of all Created things;
Look where I may, still nothing I discern
But Thee throughout this Universe, wherein
Thyself Thou dost reflect, and through those eyes
Of him whom MAN thou madest, scrutinize.
To thy Harím DIVIDUALITY
No entrance finds — no word of THIS and THAT;
Do Thou my separate and derivèd Self
Make one with thy Essential! Leave me room
On that Diván which leaves no room for Twain;
Lest, like the simple Arab in the tale,
I grow perplext, oh God! 'twixt 'ME' and 'THEE';
If *I* — this Spirit that inspires me whence?
If *THOU* — then what this sensual Impotence?

———————

From the solitary Desert
Up to Baghdád came a simple
    Arab; there amid the rout
Grew bewilder'd of the countless
People, hither, thither, running,
Coming, going, meeting, parting,
Clamour, clatter, and confusion,
    All about Him and about.

[1] The Persian Mystics also represent the Deity dicing with
Human Destiny behind the Curtain.

Travel-wearied, hubbub-dizzy,
Would the simple Arab fain
Get to sleep — 'But then, on waking,
'How', quoth he, 'amid so many
    'Waking know Myself again?'
So, to make the matter certain,
Strung a gourd about his ankle,
And, into a corner creeping,
Baghdád and Himself and People
    Soon were blotted from his brain.
    But one that heard him and divined
His purpose, slily crept behind;
From the Sleeper's ankle slipping,
    Round his own the pumpkin tied,
    And laid him down to sleep beside.
By and by the Arab waking
Looks directly for his Signal —
Sees it on another's Ankle —
Cries aloud, 'Oh Good-for-nothing
Rascal to perplex me so!
That by you I am bewilder'd,
Whether I be I or no!
If I *— the Pumpkin why on* YOU?
If YOU *— then Where am I, and* WHO?

———————

AND yet, how long, O Jámí, stringing Verse,
Pearl after pearl, on that old Harp of thine?
Year after year attùning some new Song,
The breath of some old Story?[1] Life is gone,
And that last song is not the last; my Soul
Is spent — and still a Story to be told!
And I, whose back is crooked as the Harp
I still keep tuning through the Night till Day!
That harp untuned by Time — the harper's hand
Shaking with Age — how shall the harper's hand
Repair its cunning, and the sweet old harp

———

[1] 'Yúsuf and Zulaikhá', 'Laila and Majnún', etc.

18

Be modulated as of old? Methinks
'Twere time to break and cast it in the fire;
The vain old harp, that, breathing from its strings
No music more to charm the ears of men,
May, from its scented ashes, as it burns,
Breathe resignation to the Harper's soul,
Now that his body looks to dissolution.
My teeth fall out — my two eyes see no more
Till by Feringhí glasses turn'd to four;[1]

─────────────

Pain sits with me sitting behind my knees,
From which I hardly rise unhelpt of hand;
I bow down to my root, and like a Child
Yearn, as is likely, to my Mother Earth,
Upon whose bosom I shall cease to weep,
And on my Mother's bosom fall asleep.[2]

The House in ruin, and its music heard
No more within, nor at the door of speech,
Better in silence and oblivion
To fold me head and foot, remembering
What THE VOICE whisper'd in the Master's[3] ear —
'No longer think of Rhyme, but think of ME!' —
Of WHOM? Of HIM whose Palace the SOUL is,
And Treasure-house — who notices and knows
Its income and out-going, and *then* comes
To fill it when the Stranger is departed.
Yea; but whose Shadow being Earthly Kings,
Their Attributes, their Wrath and Favour, His, —

[1] First notice of Spectacles in Oriental Poetry, perhaps.
[2] The same Figure is found in Chaucer's 'Pardoner's Tale', and, I
think, in other western poems of that era.
[3] Mohammed Saaduddin Káshgharí, spoken of in Notice of Jámí's
life, p. 8.

Lo! in the meditation of His glory,
The SHÁH[1] whose subject upon Earth I am,
As he of Heaven's, comes on me unaware,
And suddenly arrests me for his due.
Therefore the one last travel, and as brief
As may become the feeble breath of Age,
My weary Duty once more drinks of the well,
Whence, of the Mortal writing, I may read
Anticipation of the Invisible.

One who travell'd in the Desert
Saw MAJNÚN *where he was sitting*
All alone like a Magician
    Tracing Letters in the Sand.
'Oh distracted Lover! writing
What the Sword-wind of the Desert
Undeciphers so that no one
    After you shall understand'.
MAJNÚN *answer'd* — *'I am writing*
Only for myself, and only
*"*LAILA*"* — *if for ever* *"*LAILA*"*
Writing, in that Word a Volume,
Over which for ever poring,
From her very Name I sip
In Fancy, till I drink, her Lip'.

THE STORY

PART I

A SHÁH there was who ruled the realm of Yún,[2]
And wore the Ring of Empire of Sikander;
And in his reign A SAGE, of such report
For Insight reaching quite beyond the Veil,
That Wise men from all quarters of the World,

[1] YAKÚB BEG: to whose protection Jámí owed a Song of gratitude.

[2] Or 'YAVAN', Son of Japhet, from whom the country was called 'YÚNAN' — IONIA, meant by the Persians to express Greece generally. Sikander is of course, Alexander the Great.

To catch the jewel falling from his lips
Out of the secret treasure as he went,
Went in a girdle round him. — Which THE SHÁH
Observing, took him to his secresy;
Stirr'd not a step, nor set design afoot,
Without the Prophet's sanction; till, so counsell'd,
From Káf to Káf[1] reach'd his Dominion:
No People, and no Prince that over them
The ring of Empire wore, but under his
Bow'd down in Battle; rising then in Peace
Under his Justice grew, secure from wrong,
And in their strength was his Dominion strong.
The SHÁH that has not Wisdom in himself,
Nor has a Wise one for his Counsellor,
The wand of his Authority falls short,
And his Dominion crumbles at the base.
For he, discerning not the characters
Of Tyranny and Justice, confounds both,
Making the World a desert, and Redress
A fantom-water of the Wilderness.

God said to the Prophet David —
'David, whom I have exalted
From the sheep to be my People's
*   Shepherd, by your Justice my*
*   Revelation justify.*
Lest the misbelieving — yea,
The Fire-adoring Princes rather
Be my Prophets, who fulfil,
Knowing not my WORD, my WILL '.

ONE night THE SHÁH of Yúnan as he sate
Contemplating his measureless extent
Of Empire, and the glory wherewithal,
As with a garment robed, he ruled alone;

[1] The Fabulous Mountain supposed by Asiatics to surround the World, binding the Horizon on all sides.

Then found he nothing wanted to his heart
Unless a Son, who, while he lived, might share,
And, after him, his robe of Empire wear.
And then he turn'd him to THE SAGE, and said:
'O Darling of the soul of IFLATÚN;[1]
To whom with all his school ARISTO bows;

Yea, thou that an ELEVENTH to the TEN
INTELLIGENCES addest: Thou hast read
The yet unutter'd secret of my Heart;
Answer — Of all that man desires of God
Is any blessing greater than a Son?
Man's prime Desire; by whom his name and he
Shall live beyond himself; by whom his eyes
Shine living, and his dust with roses blows.
A Foot for thee to stand on, and an Arm
To lean by; sharp in battle as a sword;
Salt of the banquet-table; and a tower
Of salutary counsel in Diván;
One in whose youth a Father shall prolong
His years, and in his strength continue strong'.

When the shrewd SAGE had heard THE SHÁH'S discourse
In commendation of a Son, he said:
'Thus much of a *Good* Son, whose wholesome growth
Approves the root he grew from. But for one
Kneaded of *Evil* — well, could one revoke
His generation, and as early pull
Him and his vices from the string of Time.
Like Noah's, puff'd with insolence and pride,
Who, reckless of his Father's warning call,
Was by the voice of ALLAH from the door
Of refuge in his Father's Ark debarr'd,
And perish'd in the Deluge.[2] And as none
    Who long for children, may their children choose,
Beware of teazing Allah for a Son,
    Whom having, you may have to pray to lose'.

----

[1] Iflatún, Plato: Aristo, Aristotle: both renowned in the East to
this Day.
[2] See note in Appendix.

Sick at heart for want of Children,
Ran before the Saint a Fellow,
Catching at his garment, crying,
   'Master, hear and help me! Pray
   That ALLAH *from the barren clay*
Raise me up a fresh young Cypress,
Who my longing eyes may lighten,
And not let me like a vapour
   Unremember'd pass away'.
But the Dervish said — '*Consider;*
   Wisely let the matter rest
In the hands of ALLAH *wholly,*
Who, whatever we are after,
   Understands our business best'.
Still the man persisted — '*Master,*
I shall perish in my longing:
Help, and set my prayer a-going!'
   Then the Dervish raised his hand —
   From the mystic Hunting-land
Of Darkness to the Father's arms
   A musky Fawn of China drew —
A Boy — who, when the shoot of Passion
   In his Nature planted grew,
Took to drinking, dicing, drabbing.
From a corner of the house-top
Ill-insulting honest women,
Dagger-drawing on the husband;
   And for many a city-brawl
Still before the Cadi summon'd,
   Still the Father pays for all.
Day and night the youngster's doings
Such — the city's talk and scandal;
Neither counsel, threat, entreaty,
Moved him — till the desperate Father
Once more to the Dervish running,
Catches at his garment — crying —
'Oh my only Hope and Helper!
One more Prayer! That God, who laid,
Would take this trouble from my head!'

But the Saint replied 'Remember
How that very Day I warn'd you
Not with blind petition ALLAH
Trouble to your own confusion;
   Unto whom remains no more
To pray for, save that He may pardon
   What so rashly pray'd before'.

So much for the result; and for the means —
Oh SHÁH, who would not be himself a slave,
Which SHÁH least should, and of an appetite
Among the basest of his slaves enslaved —
Better let Azrael find him on his throne
Of Empire sitting childless and alone,
Than his untainted Majesty resign
To that seditious drink, of which one draught
Still for another and another craves,
Till it become a noose to draw the Crown
From off thy brows — about thy lips a ring,
Of which the rope is in a Woman's hand,
To lead thyself the road of Nothing down.
For what is *She?* A foolish, faithless thing —
A very Káfir in rapacity;
Robe her in all the rainbow-tinted woof
If Susa, shot with rays of sunny Gold;
Deck her with jewel thick as Night with star;
Pamper her appetite with Houri fruit
Of Paradise, and fill her jewell'd cup
From the green-mantled Prophet's Well of Life —
One little twist of temper — all your cost
Goes all for nothing: and, as for yourself —
Look! On your bosom she may lie for years;
   But, get you gone a moment out of sight,
And she forgets you — worse, if, as you turn,
   Her eyes on any younger Lover light'.

Once upon the Throne together
Telling one another Secrets,
Sate SULAYMÁN *and* BALKÍS;[1]
The Hearts of both were turn'd to Truth,
Unsullied by Deception.
First the King of Faith SULAYMÁN
  Spoke — '*However just and wise*
Reported, none of all the many
Suitors to my palace thronging
  But afar I scrutinize;
And He who comes not empty-handed
  Grows to Honour in mine Eyes'.
  After this, BALKÍS *a Secret*
From her hidden bosom utter'd,
Saying — '*Never night or morning*
Comely Youth before me passes
Whom I look not after, longing' —

'If this, as wise Firdausí says, the curse
Of better women, what then of the worse?'

THE SAGE his satire ended; and THE SHÁH,
Determined on his purpose, but the means
Resigning to Supreme Intelligence
With Magic-mighty Wisdom his own WILL
Colleagued, and wrought his own accomplishment.
For Lo! from Darkness came to Light A CHILD,
Of carnal composition unattaint;
A Perfume from the realm of Wisdom wafted;
A Rosebud blowing on the Royal stem;
The crowning Jewel of the Crown; a Star
Under whose augury triumph'd the Throne.
For whom dividing, and again in one
Whole perfect Jewel re-uniting, those

[1] Solomon and the Queen of Sheba, who, it appears, is no worse in one way than Solomon in another, unless in Oriental Eyes.

Twin Jewel-words, SALÁMAT and ASMÁN,[1]
They hail'd him by the title of SALÁMÁN.
And whereas from no Mother milk he drew,
They chose for him a Nurse — her name ABSÁL —
So young, the opening roses of her breast
But just had budded to an infant's lip;
So beautiful, as from the silver line
Dividing the musk-harvest of her hair
Down to her foot that trampled crowns of Kings,
A Moon of beauty full; who thus elect
Should in the garment of her bounty fold
SALÁMÁN of auspicious augury,
Should feed him with the flowing of her breast.
And, once her eyes had open'd upon Him,
They closed to all the world beside, and fed
For ever doating on her Royal jewel
Close in his golden cradle casketed:
Opening and closing which her day's delight,
To gaze upon his heart-inflaming cheek —
Upon the Babe whom, if she could, she would
Have cradled as the Baby of her eye.[2]
In rose and musk she wash'd him — to his lip
Press'd the pure sugar from the honeycomb;
And when, day over, she withdrew her milk,
She made, and having laid him in, his bed,
Burn'd all night like a taper o'er his head.

And still as Morning came, and as he grew,
Finer than any bridal-puppet, which
To prove another's love a woman sends,[3]
She trick'd him up — with fresh Collyrium dew
Touch'd his narcissus eyes — the musky locks
Divided from his forehead — and embraced
With gold and ruby girdle his fine waist.

[1] SALÁMAT, Security from Evil; ASMÁN, Heaven.
[2] Literally, *Mardumak* — the *Mannikin*, or *Pupil*, of the Eye, corresponding to the Image so frequently used by our old Poets.
[3] See Appendix.

So for seven years she rear'd and tended him:
Nay, when his still-increasing moon of Youth
Into the Further Sign of Manhood pass'd,
Pursued him yet, till full fourteen his years,
Fourteen-day full the beauty of his face,
That rode high in a hundred thousand hearts.
For, when SALÁMÁN was but half-lance high,
Lance-like he struck a wound in every one,
And shook down splendour round him like a Sun.

SOON as the Lord of Heav'n had sprung his horse
Over horizon into the blue field,
SALÁMÁN kindled with the wine of sleep,
Mounted a barb of fire for the Maidán;
He and a troop of Princes — Kings in blood,
Kings in the kingdom-troubling tribe of beauty,
All young in years and courage,[1] bat in hand
Gallop'd a-field, toss'd down the golden ball
And chased, so many crescent Moons a full:[2]
And, all alike intent upon the Game,
SALÁMÁN still would carry from them all
The prize, and shouting 'Hál!' drive home the ball.

This done, SALÁMÁN bent him as a bow
To Archery — from Masters of the craft
Call'd for an unstrung bow — himself the cord
Fitted unhelpt,[3] and nimbly with his hand
Twanging made cry, and drew it to his ear:
Then, fixing the three-feather'd fowl, discharged:

[1] The same Persian Word signifying Youth and Courage.
[2] See Appendix.
[3] Bows being so gradually stiffened, according to the age and
strength of the Archer, as at last to need five Hundred-weight of
pressure to bend, says an old Translation of Chardin, who describes
all the process up to bringing up the string to the ear, '*as if to hang it
there*' before shooting. Then the first trial was, who could shoot
highest: then, the mark, etc.

And whether aiming at the fawn a-foot,
Or bird on wing, direct his arrow flew,
Like the true Soul that cannot but go true.

WHEN night came, that releases man from toil,
He play'd the chess of social intercourse;
Prepared his banquet-hall like Paradise,
Summon'd his Houri-faced musicians,
And, when his brain grew warm with wine, the veil
Flung off him of reserve: taking a harp,
Between its dry string and his finger quick
Struck fire: or catching up a lute, as if
A child for chastisement, would pinch its ear
To wailing that should agéd eyes make weep.
Now like the Nightingale he sang alone;
Now with another lip to lip; and now
Together blending voice and instrument;
And thus with his associates night he spent.

His Soul rejoiced in knowledge of all kind;
The fine edge of his Wit would split a hair,
And in the noose of apprehension catch
A meaning ere articulate in word;
Close as the knitted jewel of Parwín
His jewel Verse he strung; his Rhetoric
Enlarging like the Mourners of the Bier.[1]
And when he took the nimble reed in hand
To run the errand of his Thought along
Its paper field — the character he traced,
Fine on the lip of Youth as the first hair,
Drove Penmen, as that Lovers, to despair.

[1] The Pleiades and the Great Bear. This is otherwise prettily
applied in the Anvári Soheili — 'When one grows poor, his Friends,
heretofore compact as THE PLEIADES, disperse wide asunder as THE
MOURNERS'.

His Bounty like a Sea was fathomless
That bubbled up with jewel, and flung pearl
Where'er it touch'd, but drew not back again;
It was a Heav'n that rain'd on all below
Dirhems for drops —

    But here that inward Voice
Arrested and rebuked me — 'Foolish Jámí!
Wearing that indefatigable pen
In celebration of an alien SHÁH
Whose Throne, not grounded in the Eternal World,
If YESTERDAY it were, TO-DAY is not,
TO-MORROW cannot be'.[1] But I replied;
Oh Fount of Light! — under an alien name
I shadow One upon whose head the Crown
WAS and yet IS, and SHALL BE; whose Firmán
The Kingdoms Sev'n of this World, and the Seas,
And the Sev'n Heavens, alike are subject to.
Good luck to him who under other Name
Instructed us that Glory to disguise
To which the Initiate scarce dare lift his eyes'.

Sate a Lover in a garden
All alone, apostrophizing
Many a flower and shrub about him,
   And the lights of Heav'n above.
Nightingaling thus, a Noodle
Heard him, and, completely puzzled,
'What', quoth he, 'and you a Lover,
Raving, not about your Mistress,
But about the stars and roses —
   What have these to do with Love?'

[1] The Hero of the Story being of YÚNAN — IONIA, or Greece generally (the Persian Geography not being very precise) — and so not of THE FAITH.

Answer'd he; 'Oh thou that aimest
Wide of Love, and Lovers' language
    Wholly misinterpreting;
Sun and Moon are but my Lady's
Self, as any Lover knows;
Hyacinth I said, and meant her
Hair — her cheek was in the rose —
And I myself the wretched weed
That in her cypress shadow grows'.

———————

AND now the cypress stature of Salámán
Had reached his top, and now to blossom full
The garden of his Beauty: and Absál,
Fairest of hers, as of his fellows he
The fairest, long'd to gather from the tree.
But, for the flower upon the lofty stem
Of Glory grew to which her hand fell short,
She now with woman's sorcery began
To conjure as she might within her reach.
The darkness of her eyes she darken'd round
With surma, to benight him in mid day,
And over them adorn'd and arch'd the bows[1]
To wound him there when lost: her musky locks
Into so many snaky ringlets curl'd,
In which Temptation nestled o'er the cheek
Whose rose she kindled with vermilion dew,
And then one subtle grain of musk laid there,[2]
The bird of that belovéd heart to snare.
Sometimes in passing with a laugh would break
The pearl-enclosing ruby of her lips;

[1] With dark Indigo-Paint, as the Archery Bow with a thin Papyrus-like Bark.

[2] A *Patch*, sc. — '*Noir comme le Musc*'. De Sacy.

Or, busied in the room, as by mischance
Would let the lifted sleeve disclose awhile
The vein of silver running up within:
Or, rising as in haste, her golden anklets
Clash, at whose sudden summons to bring down
Under her silver feet the golden Crown.
Thus, by innumerable witcheries,
She went about soliciting his eyes,
Through which she knew the robber unaware
Steals in, and takes the bosom by surprise.

———————

Burning with her love ZULAIKÁ
Built a chamber, wall and ceiling
Blank as an untarnisht mirror,
Spotless as the heart of YÚSUF.
Then she made a cunning painter
Multiply her image round it;
Not an inch of wall or ceiling
But re-echoing her beauty.
Then amid them all in all her
Glory sat she down, and sent for
    YÚSUF — *she began a tale*
    Of Love — and lifted up her veil.
Bashfully beneath her burning
Eyes he turn'd away; but turning
Wheresoever, still about him
Saw ZULAIKHÁ, *still* ZULAIKHÁ,
Still, without a veil, ZULAIKHÁ.
But a voice as if from Canaan
Call'd him; and a Hand from Darkness
    Touch'd; and ere a living Lip
Through the mirage of bewilder'd
Eyes seduced him, he recoil'd,
    And let the skirt of danger slip.

———————

PART II

ALAS for those who having tasted once
Of that forbidden vintage of the lips
That, press'd and pressing, from each other draw
The draught that so intoxicates them both,
That, while upon the wings of Day and Night
Time rustles on, and Moons do wax and wane,
As from the very Well of Life they drink,
And, drinking, fancy they shall never drain,
But rolling Heaven from his ambush whispers,
'So in my license is it not set down:
Ah for the sweet societies I make
At Morning, and before the Nightfall break,
Ah for the bliss that coming Night fills up,
And Morn looks in to find an empty Cup!'

————————

Once in Baghdád a poor Arab,
After weary days of fasting,
Into the Khalífah's banquet-
Chamber, where, aloft in State
HARÚN *the Great at supper sate,*
Push'd and pushing, with the throng,
Got before a perfume-breathing
Pasty, like the lip of SHÍRÍN
Luscious, or the Poet's song.
Soon as seen, the famisht clown
Seizes up and swallows down.
Then his mouth undaunted wiping —
'Oh Khalífah, hear me swear,*
While I breathe the dust of Baghdád,
Ne'er at any other Table
Than at Thine to sup or dine.'
Grimly laugh'd HARÚN, *and answer'd;*
'Fool! who think'st to arbitrate*
What is in the hands of Fate —
Take, and thrust him from the Gate!'

————————

WHILE a full Year was counted by the Moon,
SALÁMÁN and ABSÁL rejoiced together,
And neither SHÁH nor SAGE his face beheld.
They question'd those about him, and from them
Heard something: then himself to presence summon'd,
And all the truth was told. The SAGE and SHÁH
Struck out with hand and foot in his redress.
And first with REASON, which is also best;
REASON that rights the wanderer; that completes
The imperfect; REASON that resolves the knot
Of either world, and sees beyond the Veil.
For REASON is the fountain from of old
From which the Prophets drew, and none beside:
Who boasts of other inspiration, lies —
There are no other Prophets than THE WISE.

AND first THE SHÁH: — 'SALÁMÁN, Oh my Soul,
'Light of the eyes of my Prosperity,
And making bloom the court of Hope with rose;
Year after year, SALÁMÁN, like a bud
That cannot blow, my own blood I devour'd,
Till, by the seasonable breath of God,
At last I blossom'd into thee, my Son;
Oh, do not wound me with a dagger thorn;
Let not the full-blown rose of Royalty
Be left to wither in a hand unclean.
For what thy proper pastime? Bat in hand
To mount and manage RAKHSH[1] along the Field;
Not, with no weapon but a wanton curl
Idly reposing on a silver breast.
Go, fly thine arrow at the antelope
And lion — let me not My lion see
Slain by the arrow eyes of a ghazál.
Go, challenge ZÁL or RUSTAM to the Field,
And smite the warriors' neck; not, flying them,

[1] 'Lightning'. The name of RUSTAM'S famous Horse in the SHÁH-NÁMEH.

Beneath a woman's foot submit thine own.
Oh wipe the woman's henna from thy hand,
Withdraw thee from the minion[1] who from thee
Dominion draws, and draws me with thee down;
Years have I held my head aloft, and all
For Thee — Oh shame if thou prepare my Fall!'

When before SHIRÚYEH's *dagger*
  KAI KHUSRAU,[2] *his Father, fell,*
    He declared this Parable —
'Wretch! — There was a branch that waxing
Wanton o'er the root he drank from,
  At a draught the living water
    Drain'd wherewith himself to crown;
Died the root — and with him died
    The branch — and barren was brought down!'

THE SHÁH ceased counsel, and THE SAGE began.
Oh last new vintage of the Vine of Life
Planted in Paradise; Oh Master-stroke,
And all-concluding flourish of the Pen
KUN FA YAKÚN[3]; Thyself prime Archetype,
And ultimate Accomplishment of MAN!
The Almighty hand, that out of common earth
Thy mortal outward to the perfect form
Of Beauty moulded, in the fleeting dust
Inscribed HIMSELF, and in thy bosom set
A mirror to reflect HIMSELF in Thee.

---

[1] 'SHÁH', and 'SHÁHID (A Mistress).

[2] KHUSRAU PARVÍZ (Chosroe The Victorious), Son of NOSHÍRVÁN The Great; slain, after Thirty Years of prosperous Reign, by his Son SHÍRÚYEH, who, according to some, was in love with his Father's mistress SHÍRÍN. See further on one of the most dramatic Tragedies in Persian history.

[3] 'BE! AND IT IS' — The famous Word of Creation stolen from Genesis by the Kurán.

Let not that dust by rebel passion blown
Obliterate that character: nor let
That Mirror, sullied by the breath impure,
Or form of carnal beauty fore-possest,
Be made incapable of the Divine.
Supreme is thine Original degree,
Thy Star upon the top of Heaven; but Lust
Will bring it down, down even to the Dust!'

Quoth a Muezzin to the crested
Cock — 'Oh Prophet of the Morning,
*   Never Prophet like to you*
Prophesied of Dawn, nor Muezzin
With so shrill a voice of warning
Woke the sleeper to confession
Crying, "Lá allah illá 'llah,
*   Muhammad rasúluhu".[1]*
One, methinks, so rarely gifted
*   Should have prophesied and sung*
*   In Heav'n, the Birds of Heav'n among,*
Not with these poor hens about him,
*   Raking in a heap of dung.'*
'And', replied the Cock, 'in Heaven
Once I was; but by my foolish
Lust to this uncleanly living
With my sorry mates about me
*   Thus am fallen. Otherwise,*
I were prophesying Dawn
*   Before the gates of Paradise'.[2]*

---

[1] There is no God but God; Muhammad is his Prophet'.

[2] Jámí, as, may be, other Saintly Doctors, kept soberly to one Wife. But wherefore, under the Law of Muhammad, should the Cock be selected (as I suppose he is) for a '*Caution*' because of his indulgence in Polygamy, however unusual among Birds?

OF all the Lover's sorrows, next to that
Of Love by Love forbidden, is the voice
Of Friendship turning harsh in Love's reproof,
And overmuch of Counsel — whereby Love
Grows stubborn, and recoiling unsupprest
Within, devours the heart within the breast.

SALÁMÁN heard; his Soul came to his lips;
Reproaches struck not ABSÁL out of him,
But drove Confusion in; bitter became
The drinking of the sweet draught of Delight,
And waned the splendour of his Moon of Beauty.
His breath was Indignation, and his heart
Bled from the arrow, and his anguish grew.
How bear it? — By the hand of Hatred dealt,
Easy to meet — and deal with, blow for blow;
But from Love's hand which one must not requite,
And cannot yield to — what resource but Flight?
Resolved on which, he victuall'd and equipp'd
A Camel, and one night he led it forth,
And mounted — he with ABSÁL at his side,
Like sweet twin almonds in a single shell.
And Love least murmurs at the narrow space
That draws him close and closer in embrace.

———————

When the Moon of Canaan YÚSUF
In the prison of Egypt darken'd,
Nightly from her spacious Palace-
    Chamber, and its rich array,
Stole ZULAIKHÁ *like a fantom*
To the dark and narrow dungeon
    Where her buried Treasure lay.
Then to those about her wond'ring —
'Were my Palace', she replied,
'Wider than Horizon-wide,
It were narrower than an Ant's eye,

Were my Treasure not inside:
And an Ant's eye, if but there
My Lover, Heaven's horizon were'.

SIX days SALÁMÁN on the Camel rode,
And then the hissing arrows of reproof
Were fallen far behind; and on the Seventh
He halted on the Seashore; on the shore
Of a great Sea that reaching like a floor
Of rolling Firmament below the Sky's
From KÁF to KÁF, to GAU and MÁHÍ[1] down
Descended, and its Stars were living eyes.
The Face of it was as it were a range
Of moving Mountains; or a countless host
Of Camels trooping tumultuously up,
Host over host, and foaming at the lip.
Within, innumerable glittering things
Sharp as cut Jewels, to the sharpest eye
Scarce visible, hither and hither slipping,
As silver scissors slice a blue brocade;
But should the Dragon coil'd in the abyss[2]
Emerge to light, his starry counter-sign
Would shrink into the depth of Heav'n aghast.

SALÁMÁN eyed the moving wilderness
On which he thought, once launcht, no foot, nor eye

---

[1] Bull and Fish — the lowest Substantial Base of Earth. 'He first made the Mountains; then cleared the Face of the Earth from Sea; then fixed it fast on Gau; Gau on, Máhí; and Máhí on Air; and Air on what? on NOTHING; Nothing on Nothing, all is Nothing — Enough'. Attár; quoted in De Sacy's Pendnamah, xxxv.

[2] The Sidereal Dragon, whose Head, according to the Pauránic (or poetic) astronomers of the East, devoured the Sun and Moon in Eclipse. 'But *we* know', said Rámachandra to Sir W. Jones, 'that the supposed Head and Tail of the Dragon mean only the *Nodes*, or points formed by intersections of the Ecliptic and the Moon's Orbit'.
— Sir W. Jones' Works, Vol. iv., p. 74.

Should ever follow; forthwith he devised
Of sundry scented woods along the shore
A little shallop like a Quarter-moon,
Wherein Absál and He like Sun and Moon
Enter'd as into some Celestial Sign;
That, figured like a bow, but arrow-like
In flight, was feather'd with a little sail,
And, pitcht upon the water like a duck,
So with her bosom sped to her Desire.

When they had sail'd their vessel for a Moon,
And marr'd their beauty with the wind o' the Sea,
Suddenly in mid sea reveal'd itself
An Isle, beyond imagination fair;
An Isle that all was Garden; not a Flower,
Nor Bird of plumage like the flower, but there;
Some like the Flower, and others like the Leaf;
Some, as the Pheasant and the Dove adorn'd
With crown and collar, over whom, alone,
The jewell'd Peacock like a Sultan shone;
While the Musicians, and among them Chief
The Nightingale, sang hidden in the trees
Which, arm in arm, from fingers quivering
With any breath of air, fruit of all kind
Down scatter'd in profusion to their feet,
Where fountains of sweet water ran between,
And Sun and shadow chequer-chased the green.
Here Iram-garden seem'd in secresy
Blowing the rosebud of its Revelation;[1]
Or Paradise, forgetful of the dawn
Of Audit, lifted from her face the veil.

SALÁMÁN saw the Isle, and thought no more
Of Further — there with ABSÁL he sate down,
ABSÁL and He together side by side
Together like the Lily and the Rose,
Together like the Soul and Body, one.
Under its trees in one another's arms

---

[1] Note in Appendix.

They slept — they drank its fountains hand in hand —
Paraded with the Peacock — raced the Partridge —
Chased the green Parrot for his stolen fruit,
Or sang divisions with the Nightingale.
There was the Rose without a thorn, and there
The Treasure and no Serpent[1] to beware
Of; think of such a Mistress at your side
In such a Solitude, and none to chide!

Said to WÁMIK *one who never*
Knew the Lover's passion — *'Why*
Solitary thus and silent
Solitary places haunting,
Like a Dreamer, like a Spectre,
    Like a thing about to die?'
WÁMIK *answer'd* — *'Meditating*
Flight with Azrâ[2] to the Desert:
There by so remote a Fountain
That, whichever way one travell'd,
League on league, one yet should never
See the face of Man; for ever
There to gaze on my Beloved;
Gaze, till Gazing out of Gazing
Grew to Being Her I gaze on,
SHE *and I no more, but in One*
Undivided Being blended.
All that is by Nature twain
Fears, or suffers by, the pain
Of Separation: Love is only
    Perfect when itself transcends
Itself, and, one with that it loves,
    In undivided Being blends'.

----

[1] The supposed guardian of buried treasure.
[2] Wámik and Azrá (Virgin) two typical Lovers.

WHEN by and by the SHÁH was made aware
Of that heart-breaking Flight, his royal robe
He changed for ashes, and his Throne for dust,
And wept awhile in darkness and alone.
Then rose; and, taking counsel from the SAGE,
Pursuit set everywhere afoot: but none
Could trace the footstep of the flying Deer.
Then from his secret Art the Sage-Vizyr
A Magic Mirror made; a Mirror like
The bosom of All-wise Intelligence
Reflecting in its mystic compass all
Within the sev'n-fold volume of the World
Involved; and, looking in that Mirror's face,
The SHÁH beheld the face of his Desire.
Beheld those Lovers, like that earliest pair
Of Lovers, in this other Paradise
So far from human eyes in the mid sea,
And yet within the magic glass so near
As with a finger one might touch them, isled.
THE SHÁH beheld them; and compassion touch'd
His eyes and anger died upon his lips;
And arm'd with Righteous Judgment as he was,
Yet, seeing those two Lovers with one lip
Drinking that cup of Happiness and Tears[1]
In which Farewell had never yet been flung,[2]
He paused for their repentance to recall
The lifted arm that was to shatter all.

The Lords of Wrath have perish'd by the blow
Themselves had aim'd at others long ago.
Draw not in haste the sword, which Fate, may be,
Will sheathe, hereafter to be drawn on Thee.

----

[1] Κρατῆρα μακρὸν ἡδονῆς καὶ δακρύων
Κιρνῶντες ἐξέπινον ἄχρις ἐς μέθην.
(*From Theodorus Prodomus, as quoted by Sir W. Jones*)
[2] A pebble flung into a Cup being a signal for a company to break
up.

FARHÁD, *who the shapeless mountain*
Into human likeness moulded,
Under SHÍRÍN'S *eyes as slavish*
   Potters' earth himself became.

Then the secret fire of jealous
Frenzy, catching and devouring
  KAI KHUSRAU, *broke into flame.*

With that ancient Hag of Darkness
Plotting, at the midnight Banquet
FARHÁD'S *golden cup he poison'd,*
  And in SHÍRÍN'S *eyes alone*

Reign'd — But Fate that Fate revenges,
Arms SHÍRÚYEH *with the dagger*
That at once from SHÍRÍN *tore,*
  And hurl'd him lifeless from his throne.[1]

But as the days went on, and still THE SHÁH
Beheld his Son how in the Woman lost,
And still the Crown that should adorn his head,
And still the Throne that waited for his foot,
Both trampled under by a base desire,
Of which the Soul was still unsatisfied —
Then from the sorrow of THE SHÁH fell Fire;
To Gracelessness ungracious he became,
And, quite to shatter that rebellious lust,
Upon SALÁMÁN all his WILL, with all[2]

[1] One story is that Khusrau had promised that if Farhád cut through a Mountain, and brought a Stream through, Shírín should be his. Farhád was on the point of achieving his work, when Khusrau sent an old Woman (here, perhaps, purposely confounded with Fate) to tell him Shírín was dead; whereon Farhád threw himself headlong from the Rock. The Sculpture at Beysitún (or Besitún), where Rawlinson has deciphered Darius and Xerxes, was traditionally called Farhád's.

[2] He Mesmerizes him! — See also further on this Power of the WILL.

His SAGE-VIZYR'S Might-magic arm'd, discharged.
    And Lo! SALÁMÁN to his Mistress turn'd,
But could not reach her — look'd and look'd again,
And palpitated tow'rd her — but in vain!
Oh Misery! As to the Bankrupt's eyes
The Gold he may not finger! or the Well
To him who sees a-thirst, and cannot reach,
Or Heav'n above reveal'd to those in Hell!
Yet when SALÁMÁN'S anguish was extreme,
The door of Mercy open'd, and he saw
That Arm he knew to be his Father's reacht
To lift him from the pit in which he lay:
Timidly tow'rd his Father's eyes his own

    He lifted, pardon-pleading, crime-confest,
And drew once more to that forsaken Throne,
    As the stray bird one day will find her nest.

One was asking of a Teacher,
'How a Father his reputed
    Son for his should recognize?'
Said the Master, 'By the stripling,
As he grows to manhood, growing
Like to his reputed Father,
    Good or Evil, Fool or Wise.

'Lo the disregarded Darnel
With itself adorns the Wheat-field,
And for all the vernal season
    Satisfies the farmer's eye;
But the hour of harvest coming,
    And the thrasher by and by,
Then a barren ear shall answer,
    "Darnel, and no Wheat, am I".'

Yet Ah for that poor Lover! 'Next the curse
Of Love by Love forbidden, nothing worse
Than Friendship turn'd in Love's reproof unkind,
    And Love from Love divorcing' — Thus I said:

Alas, a worse, and worse, is yet behind —
    Love's back-blow of Revenge for having fled!

SALÁMÁN bow'd his forehead to the dust
Before his Father; to his Father's hand
Fast — but yet fast, and faster, to his own
Clung one, who by no tempest of reproof
Or wrath might be dissever'd from the stem
She grew to: till, between Remorse and Love,
He came to loathe his Life and long for Death.
And, as from him *She* would not be divorced,
With Her he fled again: he fled — but now,
To no such Island centred in the sea
As lull'd them into Paradise before;
But to the Solitude of Desolation,
The Wilderness of Death. And as before
Of sundry scented woods along the shore
A shallop he devised to carry them
Over the waters whither foot nor eye
Should ever follow them, he thought — so now
Of sere wood strewn about the plain of Death,
A raft to bear them through the wave of Fire
Into Annihilation, he devised,
Gather'd, and built; and, firing with a Torch,
Into the central flame ABSÁL and He
Sprung hand in hand exulting. But the SAGE
In secret all had order'd; and the Flame,
Directed by his self-fulfilling WILL,
Devouring Her to ashes, left untouch'd
SALÁMÁN — all the baser metal burn'd
And to itself the authentic Gold return'd.

PART III

FROM the Beginning such has been the Fate
Of Man, whose very clay was soak'd in tears.
For when at first of common Earth they took,
And moulded to the stature of the Soul,
For Forty days, full Forty days, the cloud
Of Heav'n wept over him from head to foot:
And when the Forty days had passed to Night,
The Sunshine of one solitary day
Look'd out of Heav'n to dry the weeping clay.[1]
And though that sunshine in the long arrear
   Of darkness on the breathless image rose,
   Yet, with the Living, every wise man knows
Such consummation scarcely shall be here!

SALÁMÁN fired the pile; and in the flame
That, passing him, consumed ABSÁL like straw,
Died his Divided Self, his Individual
Survived, and, like a living Soul from which
The Body falls, strange, naked, and alone.
Then rose his cry to Heaven — his eyelashes
Wept blood — his sighs stood like a smoke in Heaven,
And Morning rent her garment at his anguish.
And when Night came, that drew the pen across
The written woes of Day for all but him,
Crouch'd in a lonely corner of the house,
He seem'd to feel about him in the dark
For one who was not, and whom no fond word
Could summon from the Void in which she lay.

And so the Wise One found him where he sate
Bow'd down alone in darkness; and once more
Made the long-silent voice of Reason sound
In the deserted Palace of his Soul;
Until SALÁMÁN lifted up his head
To bow beneath the Master; sweet it seem'd,

---

[1] Some such Legend is quoted by De Sacy and D'Herbelot from
some Commentaries on the Kurán.

Sweeping the chaff and litter from his own,
To be the very dust of Wisdom's door,
Slave of the Firmán of the Lord of Life,
Who pour'd the wine of Wisdom in his cup,
Who laid the dew of Peace upon his lips;
Yea, wrought by Miracle in his behalf.
For when old Love return'd to Memory,
And broke in passion from his lips, THE SAGE,
Under whose waxing WILL Existence rose
From Nothing, and, relaxing, waned again,
Raising a Fantom Image of ABSÁL,
Set it awhile before SALÁMÁN's eyes,
Till, having sow'd the seed of comfort there,
It went again down to Annihilation.
But ever, as the Fantom past away,
THE SAGE would tell of a Celestial Love;
'ZUHRAH',[1] he said, 'ZUHRAH, compared with whom
That brightest star that bears her name in Heav'n
Was but a winking taper; and Absál,
Queen-star of Beauties in this world below,
But her distorted image in the stream
Of fleeting Matter; and all Eloquence,
And Soul-enchaining harmonies of Song,
A far-off echo of that Harp in Heav'n
Which Dervish-dances to her harmony'.

SALÁMÁN listen'd, and inclined — again
Entreated, inclination ever grew;
Until THE SAGE beholding in his Soul
The SPIRIT[2] quicken, so effectually
With ZUHRAH wrought, that she reveal'd herself
In her pure lustre to SALÁMÁN's Soul,
And blotting ABSÁL's Image from his breast
There reign'd instead. Celestial Beauty seen,
He left the Earthly; and, once come to know
Eternal Love, the Mortal he let go.

----

[1] 'ZUHRAH'. The Planetary and Celestial Venus.
[1] 'Maaní'. The Mystical pass-word of the Súfís, to express the transcendental New Birth of the Soul.

THE Crown of Empire how supreme a lot!
The Sultan's Throne how lofty! Yea, but not
For All — None but the Heaven-ward foot may dare
To mount — The head that touches Heaven to wear! —

When the Beloved of Royal augury
Was rescued from the bondage of ABSÁL,
Then he arose, and shaking off the dust
Of that lost travel, girded up his heart,
And look'd with undefiled robe to Heaven.
Then was his Head worthy to wear the Crown,
His Foot to mount the Throne. And then THE SHÁH
From all the quarters of the World-wide realm
Summon'd all those who under Him the ring
Of Empire wore, King, Counsellor, Amír;
Of whom not one but to SALÁMÁN did
Obeisance, and lifted up his neck
To yoke it under His supremacy.
Then THE SHÁH crown'd him with the Golden Crown,
And set the Golden Throne beneath his feet,
And over all the heads of the Assembly,
And in the ears of all, his Jewel-word
With the Diamond of Wisdom cut, and said:

'My Son,[1] the Kingdom of the World is not
Eternal, nor the sum of right desire;
Make thou the Law reveal'd of God thy Law,
The voice of Intellect Divine within
Interpreter; and considering TO-DAY
TO-MORROW's Seed-field, ere That come to bear,
Sow with the harvest of Eternity.
And, as all Work, and, most of all, the Work
That Kings are born to, wisely should be wrought,
Where doubtful of thine own sufficiency,
Ever, as I have done, consult the Wise.

[1] One sees Jámí taking advantage of his Allegorical Sháh to read a
lesson to the Living, — whose ears Advice, unlike Praise, scarce ever
reached, unless obliquely and by Fable. The Warning (and
doubtless with good reason) is principally aimed at the Minister.

Turn not they face away from the Old ways,
That were the canon of the Kings of Old;
Nor cloud with Tyranny the glass of Justice:
By Mercy rather to right Order turn
Confusion, and Disloyalty to Love.
In thy provision for the Realm's estate,
And for the Honour that becomes a King,
Drain not thy People's purse — the Tyranny
Which thee enriches at thy Subject's cost,
Awhile shall make thee strong; but in the end
Shall bow thy neck beneath thy People's hate,
And lead thee with the Robber down to Hell.
Thou art a Shepherd, and thy Flock the People,
To help and save, not ravage and destroy;
For which is for the other, Flock or Shepherd?
And join with thee True men to keep the Flock —
Dogs, if you will — but trusty — head in leash,
Whose teeth are for the Wolf, not for the Lamb,
And least of all the Wolf's accomplices.
For Sháhs must have Vizyrs — but be they Wise
And Trusty — knowing well the Realm's estate —
Knowing how far to Shá and Subject bound
On either hand — not by extortion, nor
By usury wrung from the People's purse,
Feeding their Master, and themselves (with whom
Enough is apt to make rebel)
To such a surfeit feeding as feeds Hell.
Proper in soul and body be they — pitiful
To Poverty — hospitable to the Saint —
Their sweet Access a salve to wounded Hearts;
Their Wrath a sword against Iniquity,
But at thy bidding only to be drawn;
Whose Ministers they are, to bring thee in
Report of Good or Evil through the Realm:
    Which to confirm with thine immediate Eye,
And least of all, remember — least of all,
Suffering Accuser also to be Judge,
    By surest steps up-builds prosperity'.

MEANING OF THE STORY

UNDER the leaf of many a Fable lies
The Truth for those who look for it; of this
If thou wouldst look behind and find the Fruit,
(To Which the Wiser hand hath found his way)
Have thy desire — No Tale of ME and THEE,
Though I and THOU be its Interpreters.[1]
What signifies THE SHÁH? and what THE SAGE?
And what SALÁMÁN not of Woman born?
Who was ABSÁL who drew him to Desire?
And what the KINGDOM that awaited him
When he had drawn his Garment from her hand?
What means THAT SEA? And what that FIERY PILE?
And what that Heavenly ZUHRAH who at last
Clear'd ABSÁL from the Mirror of his Soul?
Listen to me, and you shall understand
The Word that Lover wrote along the sand.[2]

THE Incomparable Creator, when this World
He did create, created first of all
The FIRST INTELLIGENCE[3] — First of a Chain
Of Ten Intelligences, of which the Last
Sole Agent is in this our Universe,
ACTIVE INTELLIGENCE so call'd; The One
Distributer of Evil and of Good,
Of Joy and Sorrow. Himself apart from MATTER,
In Essence and in Energy — He yet
Hath fashion'd all that is — Material Form,
And Spiritual, all from HIM — by HIM
Directed all, and in his Bounty drown'd.

[1] The Story is of *Generals*, though enacted by *Particulars*.
[2] See p. 18.
[3] 'These Ten Intelligences are only another Form of the Gnostic Daemones. The Gnostics held that Matter and Spirit could have no Intercourse — they were, as it were, *incommensurate*. How then,

Therefore is He that Firmán-issuing SHÁH
To whom the World was subject. But because
What He distributes to the Universe
   Another and a Higher Power supplies,
Therefore all those who comprehend aright,
   That Higher in THE SAGE will recognise.
HIS the PRIME SPIRIT that, spontaneously
Projected by the TENTH INTELLIGENCE,
Was from no womb of MATTER reproduced
A special Essence called THE SOUL OF MAN:
A Child of Heaven, in raiment unbeshamed
Of Sensual taint, and so SALÁMÁN named.

And who ABSÁL? — The Sense-adoring Body,
Slave to the Blood and Sense — through whom THE
SOUL,
Although the Body's very Life it be,
Doth yet imbibe the knowledge and delight
Of things of SENSE; and these in such a bond
United as GOD only can divide,
As Lovers in this Tale are signified.

granting this premise, was Creation possible? Their answer was a
kind of gradual Elimination. God, the "Actus Purus", created an
Aeon; this Aeon created a Second; and so on, until the Tenth Aeon
was sufficiently Material (as the Ten were in a continually
descending Series) to affect Matter, and so cause the Creation by
giving to Matter the Spiritual *Form*.

   Similarly we have in Sufism these Ten Intelligences in a corresponding Series, and for the same End.

   There are Ten Intelligences, and Nine Heavenly Spheres, of
which the Ninth is the Uppermost Heaven, appropriated to the First
Intelligence; the Eighth, that of the Zodiac, to the Second; the
Seventh, Saturn, to the Third; the Sixth, Jupiter, to the Fourth; the
Fifth, Mars, to the Fifth; the Fourth, The Sun, to the Sixth; The
Third, Venus, to the Seventh; the Second, Mercury, to the Eighth;
the First, The Moon, to the Ninth; and THE EARTH is the peculiar
Sphere of the Tenth, or lowest Intelligence, called THE ACTIVE'. —
E. B. C. — *v.* Appendix.

And what the Flood on which they sail'd, with those
Fantastic creatures peopled; and that Isle
In which their Paradise awhile they made,
And thought, for ever? — That false Paradise
Amid the fluctuating Waters found
Of Sensual passion, in whose bosom lies
A world of Being from the light of God
Deep as in unsubsiding Deluge drown'd.

And why was it that ABSÁL in that Isle
So soon deceived in her Delight, and He
Fell short of his Desire? — that was to show
How soon the Senses of their Passion tire,
And in a surfeit of themselves expire.

And what the turning of SALÁMÁN's Heart
Back to THE SHAH, and to the throne of Might
And Glory yearning? — What but the return
Of the lost SOUL to his true Parentage,
And back from Carnal error looking up
Repentant to his Intellectual Right.

And when the Man between his living Shame
Distracted, and the Love that would not die,
Fled once again — what meant that second Flight
Into the Desert, and that Pile of Fire
On which he fain his Passion with Himself
Would immolate? — That was the Discipline
To which the living Man himself devotes,

Till all the Sensual dross be scorcht away,
And, to its pure integrity return'd,
His Soul alone survives. But forasmuch
As from a darling Passion so divorced
The wound will open and will bleed anew,
Therefore THE SAGE would ever and anon
Raise up and set before Salámán's eyes
That Fantom of the past; but evermore
Revealing on Diviner, till his Soul
She fill'd, and blotted out the Mortal Love.

For what is ZUHRAH? — What but that Divine
Original, of which the Soul of Man
Darkly possesst, by that fierce Discipline
At last he disengages from the Dust,
And flinging off the baser rags of Sense,
And all in Intellectual Light array'd,
As Conqueror and King he mounts the Throne,
And wears the Crown of Human Glory — Whence,
Throne over Throne surmounting, he shall reign
One with the LAST and FIRST INTELLIGENCE.

———————————

This is the meaning of this Mystery,
Which to know wholly ponder in thy Heart,
Till all its ancient Secret be enlarged.
Enough — The written Summary I close,
And set my Seal —

THE
TRUTH
GOD ONLY
KNOWS

APPENDIX

'To thy Harím Dividuality
'No entrance finds', &c. (p. 17)

This Sufí Identification with Deity (further illustrated in the Story of Salámán's first flight) is shadowed in a Parable of Jeláluddín, of which here is an outline. 'One knocked at the Beloved's Door; and a Voice asked from within, 'Who is there?' and he answered, 'It is I'. Then the Voice said, 'This House will not hold Me and Thee'. And the Door was not opened. Then went the Lover into the Desert, and fasted and prayed in Solitude. And after a year he returned, and knocked again at the Door. And again the Voice asked, 'Who is there?' and he said, 'It is Thyself!' — 'and the Door was opened to him'.

O Darling of the Soul of Iflatún
To whom with all his school Aristo bows. (p. 22)

Some Traveller in the East — Professor Eastwick, I think — tells us that in endeavouring to explain to an Eastern Cook the nature of an *Irish Stew*, the man said he knew well enough about *'Aristo'*. *'Iflatún'*, might almost as well have been taken from *'Vol-au-vent'*.

'Like Noah's, puff'd with Insolence and Pride', &c. (p. 22)

In the Kurán God engages to save Noah and his Family, — meaning all who believed in the Warning. One of Noah's Sons (Canaan or Ham, some think) would not believe. 'And the Ark swam with them between waves like Mountains: and Noah called up to his Son, who was separated from him, saying, "Embark with us, my Son, and stay not with the Unbelievers". He answered, "I will get on a Mountain, which will secure me from the Water". Noah replied, "There is no security this Day from the Decree of God, except from him on whom he shall have Mercy". And a Wave passed between them, and he became one of those who were drowned. And it was said, "O Earth, swallow up they waters; and Thou, O Heaven, withhold thy Rain!" And immediately the Water abated, and the Decree was fulfilled, and the Ark rested on the Mountain Al Judi; and it was said, "Away with the ungodly People!" and Noah called upon his Lord, and said, "O Lord, verily my Son is of my Family; and thy Promise is True: for Thou art the most just of those who exercise Judgment". God answered, "O Noah, verily he is not of thy Family: this intercession of thine for him, is not a righteous work".' — *Sale's Kurán*, vol. ii. p. 21.

'Finer than any bridal-puppet, which
'To prove another's love a woman sends', &c. (p. 26)

In Atkinson's version of the 'Kitábi Kulsúm Naneh' [c. XII.] we find among other Ceremonials and Proprieties of which the Book treats, that when a Woman wished to ascertain another's Love, she sent a Doll on a Tray with flowers and sweetmeats, and judged how far her affection was reciprocated by the Doll's being returned to her drest in a Robe of Honour, or in Black. The same Book also tells of *two* Dolls — Bride and Bridegroom, I suppose — being used on such occasions; the test of Affection being whether the one sent were returned with or without its Fellow.

'The Royal Game of Chúgán'. (p. 27)

For centuries the Royal Game of Persia, and adopted (Ouseley thinks) under varying modifications of name and practice by other nations, was played by horsemen, who, suitably habited, and armed with semicircular-headed Bats or Sticks, strove to drive a Ball through a Goal of upright Pillars. We may call it 'Horse-hockey', as heretofore played by young Englishmen in the Maidán of Calcutta, and other Indian cities, I believe, and now in England itself under the name of Polo.

The Muezzin's Cry. (p. 35)

I am informed by a distinguished Arabic Scholar that the proper Cry of the Muezzin is, with some slight local variations, such as he heard it at Cairo and Damascus:

Allah Akbar, Allah Akbar;
Allah Akbar, Allah Akbar;
Ishad lá allah illá 'llah;
Ishhad lá allah illá 'llah;
Ishhad lá allah illá 'llah;
Ishhad Muhammad rasúluhu;
Ishhad Muhammad rasúluhu;
Ishhad Muhammad rasúluhu;
Hayá 'ala 's-salát, Hayá 'alá 's-salát,
Inna 's-salát khair min an-naum.

'God is great' (*four times*); 'Confess that there is no God but God', (*three times*); 'Confess that Muhammad is the prophet of God', (*three times*); 'Come to Prayer, Come to Prayer, for Prayer is better than Sleep'.
[A more accurate account will be found in Lane's Modern Egyptians.]

The Garden of Iram. (p. 38)

'Here Iram-garden seem'd in secrecy
'Blowing the rosebud of its Revelation';

'Mahomet', says Sir W. Jones, 'in the Chapter of The Morning, towards the end of his Alcoran, mentions a Garden called "Irem", which is no less celebrated by the Asiatic Poets than that of the Hesperides by the Greeks. It was planted, as the Commentators say, by a king named Shedád', — deep in the Sands of Arabia Felix — 'and was once seen by an Arabian who wandered far into the Desert in search of a lost Camel'.

The Ten Intelligences. (p. 48)

A curious parallel to this doctrine is quoted by Mr. Morley (Critical Miscellanies, Series II. p. 318), from so anti-gnostic a Doctor as Paley, in Ch. III. of his Natural Theology.

'As we have said, therefore, God prescribes limits to his power, that he may let in the exercise, and thereby exhibit demonstrations, of his wisdom. For then — *i.e.,* such laws and limitations being laid down, it is as though one Being should have fixed certain rules; and, if we may so speak, provided certain materials; and, afterwards, have committed to another Being, out of these materials, and in subordination to these rules, the task of drawing forth a Creation; a supposition which evidently leaves room, and induces indeed a necessity, for contrivance. Nay, there may be many such Agents, and many ranks of these. We do not advance this as a doctrine either of philosophy or religion; but we say that the subject may be safely represented under this view; because the Deity, acting himself by general laws, will have the same consequence upon our reasoning, as if he had prescribed these laws to another'.

———————

II

THE NICHE FOR LIGHTS

ACKNOWLEDGMENT

I HAVE greatly profited from hints, generously lavished in the course of correspondence, from Professors D. B. MACDONALD, R. NICHOLSON, and LOUIS MASSIGNON, in addition to recent works by the last two. My cordial thanks to these; and also to Professor D. S. MARGOLIOUTH for discussing with me some of the difficult points in the translation.

AUTHOR'S PREFACE

I AM so conscious that my general equipment was insufficient to warrant my having undertaken an *introduction* to this treatise (in addition to the translation), that my utmost hope is this — that what I have written may be regarded by lenient Orientalists as something to elicit — provoke, if you will — the necessary supplementing and formative criticism; or as useful materials to be built into some more authoritative and better informed work: and that they may from this point of view be inclined to pardon what otherwise might seem an unwarrantable piece of rashness and indiscretion.

A still greater presumption remains to be forgiven, but this time on the ground of the great human simplicities, when I venture to inscribe this work, in spite of everything, to the beloved memory of

IGNAZ GOLDZIHER

— that golden-hearted man — who in 1911 introduced me to the Mishkāt; and to join with his name that of

DUNCAN BLACK MACDONALD,

who first introduced me to the Mishkāt's author. Of these twain, the latter may perhaps forgive the lapses of a pupil because of the filial joy with which, I know well, he will see the two names joined together, howsoever or by whomsoever it was done. As for the former, . . . in Abraham's bosom all things are forgiven.

CAIRO
July, 1923

INTRODUCTION

[Ghazzālī's sections and titles have been supplemented. The page-references enclosed within square brackets in the Introduction, Translation, and foot-notes are references to the pages of the Arabic text,[1] the numbers of which will be found in the text of the translation, enclosed in square brackets.]

THE MISHKAT AL-ANWAR[1] is a work of extreme interest from the viewpoint of al-Ghazzālī's[2] inner life and esoteric thought. The glimpses it gives of that life and thought are remarkably, perhaps uniquely, intimate. It begins where his autobiographical *Al-Munqidh min al-Dalāl* leaves off. Its esotericism excited the curiosity and even the suspicion of Muslim thinkers from the first, and we have deeply interesting allusions to it in Ibn Tufail[3] and Ibn Rushd,[4] the celebrated philosophers of Western Islam, who flourished within the century after al-Ghazzālī's death in 1111 (A.H. 505) — a fact which, again, increases its importance and interest for us.

I. DATE, OBJECT, AND GENERAL CONTENTS

There is no way of fixing the precise date of this treatise; but it falls among his later ones, perhaps among the latest; the most important hint we get from Ghazzālī himself being that the book was written after his *magnum opus*, the *Iḥyā' al-'Ulūm* (p. [9]). Other works of Ghazzālī

---

[1] The *Mishkāt al-Anwār* is numbered No. 34 in Brockelmann's *Geschichte der Arabischen Literatur* (vol. i, p. 423). It was printed in Cairo (Maṭba'at aṣ Ṣidq. A.H. 1322), to which edition the references in the present work are made. There is another edition in a collection of five opuscules of Ghazzālī under the title of the first of the five, *Faiṣal al-Tafriqa*.

[2] The Algazal of the Schoolmen.

[3] The Abubacer of the Schoolmen.

[4] The Averroes of the Schoolmen.

mentioned by him in this treatise are the *Mī'ār al-'Ilm,
Maḥakk al-Naẓar*, and *al-Maqṣad al-Asnā*.

The object of the opuscule is to expound a certain
Koran verse and a certain Tradition. The former is the
celebrated Light-Verse (S. 24, 35) and the latter the
Veils-Tradition. It is divided into three sections, of which
the first is considerably the longest.

In this first section he considers the word "light" itself,
and its plural "lights", as applied to physical light and
lights; to the eye; to the intelligence (i.e. intellect or
reason); to prophets; to supernal beings; and finally to
Allāh himself, who is shown to be not only the source of
light and of these lights, but also the only real actual light
in all existence.

In the second section we have some most interesting
prolegomena to the whole subject of symbolic language
in the Koran and Traditions, and its interpretation.
Symbols are shown to be no mere metaphors. There is a
real mystical nexus between symbol and symbolized,
type and antitype, outer and inner. The symbols are in-
finitely numerous, very much more numerous than those
mentioned in Koran or Traditions. *Every* object on earth
"perhaps" has its correlative in the unseen, spiritual
world. This doctrine of symbols reminds us of the
Platonic "ideas" and their earthly copies, and of the
"patterns of things in the heavens" and "the example
and shadow [on earth] of heavenly things" in the Epistle
to the Hebrews. A notable deduction is made from this
doctrine, namely, the equal incumbency of keeping the
outward letter (*ẓāhir*) of the Law as well as its inner
meaning (*bāṭin*). Nearly all the most advanced Ṣūfīs were
zealous and minutely scrupulous keepers of the ritual,
ceremonial, and other prescriptions of the Sunna law,
and Ghazzālī here supplies a quasiphilosophical basis for
this fidelity — a fidelity which some of the bolder and
more extreme mystics found illogical and "unspiritual".

In the third section the results of this symbolology are
applied to the Verse and Tradition in question. In the
former the beautiful, and undeniably intriguing, expres-

sions of the Koran — the Light, the Niche, the Glass, the Oil, Tree, the East and the West — are explained both on psychological and religio-metaphysical lines; and a similar exegesis is applied to the tradition of the Seventy Thousand Veils.

II. Mysteries left Veiled in this Treatise

In the course of all this Ghazzālī gives us, incidentally, much that excites our curiosity to the highest degree; though always, when we get to the crucial point, we meet a "perhaps", or a patronizing allusion to the immaturity of his less-initiated reader. (Ghazzālī's hesitations — "it may be", "perhaps", etc. — are worthy of study in this treatise. They do not so much have the impression of hesitancy in his own mind, as of a desire to "fence" a little with his reader.) He himself writes "incommunicable mystery" across a number of these passages. Thus, the nature of the human intelligence and its peculiar affinity to the divine (pp. [6, 7]); the mystic "state" of al-Ḥallāj, and other "inebriates", and the expressions they emit in their mystic intoxication (p. [20]) — "behind which truths", says Ghazzālī, "also lie secrets which it is not lawful to enter upon"; the astounding passage (p. [24]) in which to the supreme Adept of the mystical Union with deity are ascribed features and functions of very deity; the real explanation of the word *tawḥid*, involving as it does the question of the reality of the universe and the nature of the soul's union or identification with deity; the universe, and whether he be Allāh or an ineffable supreme Vicegerent; who that Vicegerent is, and why it must be *he* and *not* Allāh who performs the prime function of the cosmosruler, viz. the issue of the command for the moving of the *primum mobile*, whereby all the motions of the Heavenly (and the Sublunary) spheres are set a-going; and the final mystery of Allāh-*an-sich*, a Noumenal Deity, in whose case transcendence is to be carried to such a pitch that gnosticism and agnosticism meet, and the validity of every possible or conceivable prediction is denied, whether of act or attribute (see p. [55]) — all these things are incommunicable mysteries, secrets, from the revealing of which our author turns away at the exact moment when we expect the *dénouement*. The art is supreme — but something more than tantalizing. Who were the adepts to whom he *did* communicate these thrilling secrets? Were these communications ever written down for or by his brother initiates? Or did he ever communicate them? Was there really anything to communicate? If so, what?

III. A GHAZZALIAN PHILOSOPHY OF RELIGION

On the whole it is the final section on the Veils Tradition which, though really of the nature of an appendix, contains the most numerous and the most interesting problems for the study of Ghazzālī's inner life, thought, and convictions. This tradition speaks of "Seventy Thousand Veils of Light and Darkness" which veil pure Godhead from the human soul. The origin of the tradition is, it is safe to hazard, Neoplatonic, and it therefore lent itself completely to the gnostic and theosophical mode of thought which so soon invaded Muslim Ṣūfism, after its less successful effort to capture orthodox Christianity. Accordingly Muslim mystics seem to have seized upon the tradition with avidity, though they interpret it variously. For an entirely Neoplatonic, theosophical interpretation, as expounded by Rifā'ī dervishes, the translator's " 'Way' of a Mohammedan Mystic" may be consulted.[1] According to this version, the soul, in its upward Seven-fold Way to Union with pure Deity, is at every stage stripped of 10,000 of these Veils, the dark ones first and then the bright. After that the naked soul stands face to face with naked Deity, with Absolute Being, with an unveiled Sun, with unadulterated Light. Ghazzālī's treatment is different. According to him, these Veils are various according to

---

[1] *The Moslem World*, year 1912, pp. 171 seqq., 245 seqq.; as separatum, Otto Harrassowitz, pp. 9, 10.

the varieties of the natures which they veil from the One Real. And it is the classification of these natures, which is thus involved, that supplies rich material for an unusually *inside* view of Ghazzālī's real views concerning men, doctrines, religions, and sects. It is not the orthodox schoolman, the fierce dogmatist, the rigid *mutakallim*, who is now speaking. We have the sensation of overhearing Ghazzālī as he speaks aloud to his own soul, or to a circle of initiates. It is hardly less than an outline of a philosophy of religion with which we have to do. He divides mankind into four classes: those veiled with veils of pure darkness; those veiled with veils of mixed darkness and light; those veiled with veils of pure light; and those who attain to the vision of the Unveiled. Every line of this part of the work merits and requires the closest study. It is not possible to give this detailed study here — it has been given elsewhere, and to that the reader must be referred.[1] But a summary of Ghazzālī's classification of souls and creeds may be given here, for thus, even more effectively than by an extended study, may a vivid preliminary appreciation be gained of the importance of this section for students of the Ghazzālī problem. He begins at the bottom and works up the light-ladder, rung by rung, to the very top, thus giving a gradation of human natures and human creeds in respect of their approach to absolute truth. Sometimes the grades are definitely identified by the author. In other cases they may be certainly, or nearly certainly identified from the description he gives. In the following summary Ghazzālī's *own* identifications are given between round brackets; *inferred* identifications, certain or nearly certain, between square brackets.

Class I. — Those veiled with Veils of pure Darkness
Atheists — (*a*) Naturist philosophers whose god is Nature,
      (*b*) Egotists whose god is Self.

[1] *Der Islām*, year 1914, in Nos. 2 and 3; by the present writer.

Subdivisions of (b):

(1) Seekers after sensual pleasures (the *bestial* attributes).
(2) Seekers after dominion ("Arabs, some Kurds, and very numerous Fools") (the *ferocious* attributes).
(3) Seekers after filthy lucre
(4) „ vainglory

Class II. – Those veiled with Veils of mixed Darkness and Light

A. THOSE WHOSE DARKNESS ORIGINATES IN THE SENSES

(1) Image-worshippers.
[Polytheists of the Hellenic (? and Indian) type.]
(2) Worshippers of animate objects of physical beauty. (Some of the most remote Turkish tribes.)
(3) Fire-worshippers.
[Magians.]
(4) Astrologizing Star-worshippers.
[Star-worshippers of Ḥarrān: ? Ṣābīans.]
(5) Sun-worshippers.
(6) Light-worshippers, with their dualistic acknowledgment of a supreme correlative Darkness. (Zoroastrians of the cult of Ormuzd and Ahrimān.)

B. THOSE WHOSE DARKNESS ORIGINATES IN THE IMAGINATION

(who worship a One Being, sitting [spatially] on his throne).

(1) Corporealists.
[Extreme Ḥanbalites: Ẓahirites.]
(2) Karrāmites.
(2) Those who have eliminated all spatial ideas in regard to Allāh except the literal "up-above".
[Ibn Ḥanbal.[1] Ḥanbalites.[2]]

[1] *Faiṣal al-Tafriqa*, p. 10.

[2] Averroes adds to these (with justice) the Koran; Mohammed himself; the "Early Fathers"; al-Ashʿari; and the early Ashʿarites "before the time of Abul Maʿālī", says Averroes, loc. cit., i.e. of al-Juwaīnī, the Imām al-Ḥaramain, our author's Shaikh, d. 478 (see his *al-Kashfʿan manāhij al-adillāʾ*, ed. Müller, p. 65, Cairo ed., p. 54).

C. Those whose Darkness Originates in the [Discursive][1] Intelligence

[Various sorts of *Mutakallimīn*]

(1) Anthropomorphists in respect of the Seven Attributes of Allāh, "Hearing, Seeing", etc., and especially the "Word" of Allāh.

(Those who said that the Word of Allāh has letters and sounds like ours.) [Early literalists; Hanbalites: early Ash'arites].

(2) Those who said that the word of Allāh is like our mental speech (*ḥadith al-nafs*).

[Later Ash'arites].

Class III. – Those veiled by pure Light

[i.e. purged of all anthropomophism (*tashbīh*)].

(1) Those whose views about the Attributes were sound, but who refused to define Allāh by means of them: replying to the question "What is the Lord of the Worlds?" by saying, "The Lord; who transcends the ideas of those attributes; He, the Mover and Orderer of the Heavens".

[Ḥasan al-Baṣrī, al-Shāfi'ī, and others of the *bilā kaifa* school].

(2) Those who mounted higher than the preceding, in declaring that Allāh is the mover of only the *primum mobile* (the Ninth and outermost Heaven), which causes the movement of the other Eight, mediated by their respective Angels.

[Ṣūfī philosophers. (?) Al Fārābī].

(3) Those who mount higher than these again, in putting a supreme Angel in place of Allāh. Who now moves the heavens by *commanding* this supreme Angel, but not immediately by direct action.

[Ṣūfī philosophers. Al-Ghazzālī himself when *coram populo* (*Munqidh*, p. 11)!]

---

[1] For according to Ghazzālī the genuine axiomata of the pure intelligence are infallible. See p. [10], and an important autobiographical passage near the beginning of the *Munqidh*.

Class IV. – The Unveiled, who Attain

Those who will predicate *nothing whatsoever* of Allāh, and refuse to allow that He even issues the order for the moving of the *primum mobile*. This Commander (*Muṭā'*) is now a Vicegerent, who is related to the Absolute Being as the sun to Essential Light or live coal to the Element of Fire.

(1) Adepts who preserve self-consciousness in their absorption in this Absolute, all else being effaced.

(2) Adepts whose self-consciousness is *also* effaced ("the Fewest of the Few")

[al-Ḥallāj and the extreme Mystics],

  (*a*) who attain to this State with a single leap — as Abraham "al-Khalīl" did,

  (*b*) who attain to it by stages, — as Mohammed "al-Ḥabīb" did [at the *Mi'rāj*].

IV. GHAZZALI PROBLEMS RAISED BY THE FOREGOING

The mere perusal of this graded scale of systems and of souls shows at once its extraordinary interest because of its revelation of Ghazzālī's innermost thought about these things; and because of the piquancy and difficulty of some of the problems raised. In the discussion of the whole subject the reader is referred to the monograph upon the *Mishkāt* to which allusion has been made. The problems may be indicated here in the form of questions, for the sake of defining them as particularly as possible:

(1) How is it that some reputable Moslems are grouped with Idolators and Dualists in the second division ("mixed light and dark")?

(2) How is it that Jews and Christians are neither mentioned nor alluded to in this rather full sketch for a philosophy of religion? And where could they have been fitted in if they had been mentioned?

(3) How is it that the later Ash'arites, the standard orthodox Theologians, are placed so low, viz. in the division where there are still veils *of darkness*?

(4) How is that the Mu'tazilites are neither mentioned nor alluded to; and that, according to the differentia of

the highest section of the second division, it would be inevitable to place them *above* the orthodox Ash'arites?

(5) How is it that the most pious believers of the earliest and most venerated type come no higher than the *lowest* section of the third division?

(6) How is it that to such men is ascribed *any* special concern about Allāh as *"mover of the Heavens"*[1]?

(7) How is it that the various doctrines about the mode of this Moving of the Heavens is made the main if not the sole differentia of the (*ascending*) grades of this division, though in other works Ghazzālī treats this very matter with marked coolness[2]? How is it that on *this* is explicitly said to turn the superiority of the schools of Ṣūfī's over the pious Believers, and the superiority of one school of Ṣūfī's over another?

(8) How is it that this matter of Moving the Heavens is considered so particularly to threaten the Unity of Allāh, and that that Unity is only saved when He is relieved from even the function of Commanding the (outer-most) Heaven to be moved?

(9) *And who is this Commander who thus commands, and who orders all things, and who is related to pure Being as the Sun to Elemental Light?* And what was "the mystery (in this affair), the disclosure of which this book does not admit of"?

(10) What becomes of a Deity of whom nothing whatsoever can even be said or predicated? And how, then, can a "relation" between Him and His Vicegerent be asserted, still more described as above? And how can this Unknowable, Unimaginable, and Inconceivable be nevertheless "reached" by mystic souls?

(11) What was "the book" into which Ghazzālī himself says he put all his esoteric teaching (*Jawāhir*, p. 31); which he implores any into whose hands it may fall not to publish; which Ibn Ṭufail denies could have

---

[1] This is all the more marked because the words italicized are Ghazzālī's own gloss on a quotation from the Koran; see below.

[2] E.g. *Tahāfut*, pp. 57, 60.

been this *Mishkāt* (*Ḥayy*, ed. Gautier, pp. 13–15, trans. Gautier, pp. 12–14), nor any other of the supposed esoteric books that "had come to Andalus"?

V. The Problem of the Vicegerent in Ibn Rushd and Ibn Ṭufail

After this it will cause no surprise that it is this figure of the Vicegerent (*al-Muṭā'* . . . *alladhī amara bi taḥrīk il-samāwāt*) who excited the curiosity and suspicion of thinkers in the century after Ghazzālī's death. The passage is at least twice singled out, once by Ibn Rushd in the treatise already cited, and once by Ibn Ṭufail in his *Ḥayy ibn Yaqẓān*.

(1) Ibn Rushd uses the passage to level at Ghazzālī a direct accusation of gravest hypocritical insincerity over a matter which Ghazzālī had ostentatiously singled out as the prime test of orthodoxy, namely, the doctrine of *emanation*. According to Ibn Rushd the passage about the Vicegerent was the explicit teaching of this doctrine of the Philosophers, for which, elsewhere, Ghazzālī can find no words strong enough to express his censure and contempt. The words of Ibn Rushd are as follows:

"Then he comes on with his book known as *Mishkāt al-Anwār*, and mentions therein all the grades of the Knowers of Allāh; and says that all of them are veiled save those who believe that Allāh is not the mover of the First Heaven, *He being the One from Whom this mover of the First Heaven emanated*: which is an open declaration on his part of the tenet of the philosophers' schools in the science of theology; though he has said in several places that their science of theology (as distinct from their other sciences) is a set of conjectures".[1]

It is not within the scope of this Introduction to follow in detail the evidence for and against the truth of this radical accusation. This has been done at length and with considerable minuteness in the monograph in *Der Islām*, which has already been cited (pp. 133–145). The

---

[1] Op. cit., ed. Müller, p. 21, Cairo edition, p. 59. The treatise was written before A.H. 575; date of *Mishkāt c.* 500.

reader must be referred to that; and it must suffice here to say that after the full consideration of all the evidence the verdict given there is Not Guilty. On the other hand, the existence of an esoteric doctrine in regard to this Vicegerent and his function is undeniable (and undenied); and it is clear, from the comparison of the *Mishkāt* itself with the *Munqidh*, that that doctrine differed vitally from the one professed by Ghazzālī exoterically (*Munqidh*, p. 11). Ghazzālī himself, in a passage of remarkable candour,[1] admits that every "Perfect" man has three sets of opinions (*madhāhib*), (*a*) those of his own environment, (*b*) those he teaches to inquirers according as they are able to receive them, and (*c*) those which he believes in secret between himself and Allāh, and never mentions except to an inner circle of friends or students.

Ibn Rushd's accusation was an attempt to identify the figure of the Vicegerant, *al-Muṭā'*, with that of *Al Ma'lūl al Awwal*, the First Caused, in the emanational scheme of the Neoplatonizing[2] philosophers of Islam, with al-Fārābī and Ibn Sīnā at their head. This was the Demiurge, the Being who first emanates from the Absolute Being, and mediates between It and all the lower stages of relational existence, with their increasing limitedness and grossness, thus relieving the predicateless Absolute from all part in the creation *or administration* of the universe.

There can be no doubt that whatever Ghazzālī's doctrine of the Vicegerent was, and whatever else his esoteric doctrine contained, the emanational theory formed no part of that doctrine. For this particular piece of pseudometaphysics he appears to have had a very particular dislike and contempt; and if Ibn Rushd was really

[1] *Mīzān al'Amal*, p. 214.

[2] The unquestionable Neoplatonism of much of the forms and expressions of Ghazzālī's thought, if not of the thought itself (see especially pp. [15, 16, 29, 47 seq.]), exposed him in a very special way to this charge of emanational pantheism. And it cannot have made it easier for him to steer clear of such dangers in fact.

serious in levelling his accusation he can hardly be acquitted of being blinded by his bitter prejudice against "Abu Ḥāmid". The only possible ground for Ibn Rushd's accusation which I have been able to discover is as follows: it is a fact that the extreme (*ghulāt*) Imāmites did identify *al-Rūḥ* "The Spirit of Allāh" with the First Emanation.[1] If, as is contended hereafter, Ghazzālī identified *al-Muṭā'* with *al-Rūḥ*, and Ibn Rushd was aware of this, he may have thought, or been pleased to think, that Ghazzālī therefore thought that *al-Muṭā'* was the First Emanation. This would be an indirect confirmation of the identification which it is attempted presently to prove, namely, *al-Muṭā'* = *al-Rūḥ*.

(2) We now pass to the other criticism of the passage, by Ibn Rushd's contemporary Ibn Ṭufail, in the introduction to his philosophical romance entitled *Ḥayy ibn Yaqẓān*.[2]

Ibn Ṭufail's allusion to this perplexing passage is as follows:

> "Some later writers[3] have fancied they have found something tremendous in that passage of his that occurs at the end of *al-Mishkāt*, which (they think) impales Ghazzālī on a dilemma from which there is no escape. I mean where, after speaking of the various degrees of the Light-Veiled, and then going on to speak of the true Attainers, he tells us that these Attainers have discovered that this Existing One possesses an attribute which negates unmitigated Unity; insisting that it necessarily follows from this that Ghazzālī believed that the Absolute Being has within His Essence some sort of plurality: which God forbid!"

The excursus on this passage in the article cited from *Der Islām* (pp. 145–151) can only be summarized here. It seems to have escaped the critics quoted by Ibn Ṭufail, that the Unveiled, according to Ghazzālī himself, *aban-*

---

[1] Massignon, *Ḥallāj*, p. 661.

[2] Ed. Gautier, pp. 13–15, transl. 12–14.

[3] Or "a later writer", presumably Ibn Rushd himself, in the passage already cited and discussed.

doned the position of the last of the Light-Veiled just because of this dread, viz. that the identification of *al-Muṭāʿ* with Allāh would endanger "the unmitigated Unity" of Deity. Ibn Ṭufail himself, though he admits the serious contradictions which appear in Ghazzālī's books, flatly refuses to see in this passage anything so monstrous, or anything sinister at all.

Unfortunately he does not give us his own exegesis of the passage; but it may perhaps be inferred from his own schematization of the grades of being. In this he makes elaborate use of the schema of reflectors, and reflectors of reflectors, which Ghazzālī has already suggested in this book (pp. [15, 16]). "The essences of the Intelligences of the Spheres" are represented as successive, graded reflections of the Divine Essence. The highest of them "is not the essence of the One Real nor is he the Sphere itself, nor is he other than both. He is, as it were, the image of the sun which appears in a polished mirror; for that image is neither the sun, nor the mirror, nor other than them both". It is probable that Ibn Ṭufail, who professed to have won through to his position after studying al-Ghazzālī and Ibn Sīnā (the juxtaposition is singular!), would have more or less equated this conception of the highest Essence of the Intelligences of the Spheres with the conception of *al-Muṭāʿ* in the *Mishkāt*, though he says nothing about the business of Heaven-moving in relation to this Being. It need not follow that al-Ghazzālī would have accepted this explanation[1]; though both men were evidently striving equally to avoid a total pantheism, and both disbelieved in the emanational theory as taught by al-Fārābī and Ibn Sīnā.

VI. One Solution of the Problem of the Vicegerent

In the absence of "the book" into which Ghazzālī put these secret opinions, or inconceivable mysteries, including, we may suppose, the secret of this mysterious

---

[1] Though his "mirror" schema in *Mishkāt*, p. [15], is near Ibn Ṭufail's meaning.

Vicegerent, we are not likely to reach any authoritative settlement of the question: nor, even if we be put on the right track, clear up the whole of the mystery. For want of direct help from our author, therefore, the only thing to be done is to examine minutely *al-Mishkāt* itself, to see if it yields any indirect help. It would seem that from this examination two possible solutions emerge. In this section the first of these will be discussed.

This solution, which was first suggested to the writer by the distinguished French Orientalist, M. Louis Massignon, identifies the mysterious figure of this Vicegerent, *al-Muṭā'*, with the *Quṭb* ("Axis") or some other Supreme Adept. According to the developed doctrine, this *Quṭb* was an earthly Mystic of supremest attainment, who during his lifetime administered the affairs of the heavens and the earth. There was nothing about him, during his lifetime, to suggest to any observer that he was engaged in so stupendous a task, and it was not known till after his death that he had been "the Axis of his time" (*quṭbu zamānihi*).

The beginnings of this doctrine go back far beyond al-Ghazzālī — a rudimentary form of it was held by even the ultra-orthodox Ḥanbalites,[1] and a developed form of the conception is expressed quite definitely in al-Hujwīrī's *Kashf al-Maḥjūb*,[2] and must have been widely held, in orthodox circles too, in the fifth century, at the close of which our treatise was written.

Moreover, at least from the time of al-Ḥallāj, to whom, as we shall see, our author in this treatise refers in terms by no means of repudiation, the very word under discussion, *al-Muṭā'*, or some other form of the same verb, occurs in significant connexion with supreme sainthood. One of the accusations levelled against al-Ḥallāj was that he taught that "having attained to sainthood the Adept becomes *al-Muṭā'*, he who says to a thing 'Be!' and it

[1] Massignon, *Passion d'al-Ḥallāj*, p. 754.
[2] P. 214 of trans.

becomes".[1] It sounds startling enough, but it was a true accusation, though it has to be taken in connexion with the whole of Ḥallāj's philosophy of mystical union with the Divine.[2] For he did definitely adopt from a predecessor, Ibn 'Iyāḍ, the aphorism "*Man aṭā'a Allaha aṭā'ahu kullu shay'*",[3] an aphorism which received a later redaction (quite in the spirit of Ḥallāj, has been shown), "*man hudhdhiba ... fa yaṣīru muṭā'an, yaqūlu lish shay'i 'Kun' fa yakūn*", "He who has passed through the mystic askesis becomes Obeyed; he says to this or that, 'Be!' and it is".[4]

Since then al-Ḥallāj did so teach, and did use this very word, and since al-Ghazzālī in this treatise betrays a very considerable admiration of al-Ḥallāj, and a sort of tremulous half-assent to his wildest utterances, including the notorious "*Ana-l Ḥaqq*" itself, it would seem that a strong prima-facie case has been made out for identifying the *Muṭā'* of our treatise, in spite of the cosmic nature of his functions, with some supreme Adept. But only a prima-facie case. To make out the thesis itself, the treatise itself must be interrogated; for it by no means follows that because a Ḥallāj held an opinion a Ghazzālī adopted it.

There are, certainly, some passages that do suggest that the solution is along this line.

(1) The description of the adventures of a soul in highest state of Union (*Mish.*, p. [24]) tends to bear out the identification, or the general idea underlying it. The person there described is a supreme Adept, and in particular al-Ḥallāj himself. Having reached Union with the One divine Real, he ascends in and with Him "to the throne of the Divine Unity and from thenceforth ad-

[1] Massignon, op. cit., p. 791; ib., p. 472.

[2] The sense in which he *did* use the expression, and the proof that it did not in his thought mean self-deification, is given very clearly in Massignon, op. cit., pp. 519–521.

[3] Op. cit., p. 472.

[4] *Al-Aynī on al-Istakhrī*; quoted in a letter by M. Massignon to the writer.

ministers the Command throughout His (or 'his', for in this extraordinary passage the pronouns remain the same throughout) storied Heavens". The words translated "administers the Command", *yudabbiru-l amr*, are remarkable, for they contain an Arabic word (*amr*) which, as we shall see presently, is to the last degree significant, being the very word used in the *Muṭāʿ* passage (p. [55]), where Ghazzālī confesses it is an obscure mystery. The *Muṭāʿ* (Commander) is said to move the outermost Heaven by precisely the *amr* (command). The words *yudabbiru-l amr* could no doubt be translated in a less significant way, owing to the troublesome double meaning of *amr* ("affair", "command"), namely, "he disposes things". But in view of the fact that this *amr* was a notable Ṣūfī term, and a mysterious problem alluded to by Ghazzālī in this very treatise, it seems inevitable to take it as "command" here. And a "Command" necessitates an "Obeyed".

(2) On p. [23], where the reference throughout is purely general, and presumably applies to *anyone* who has the necessary qualifications and attains this supreme mystical "state", Ghazzālī says that when the mystic Ascent is complete, "if there be indeed any change, it is by way of 'the Descent into the Lowest Heaven', the radiation from above downwards". This also suggests supreme divine activity in the Universe below, especially if the word *ishrāq* refers, as it probably does, to causative activity.

(3) On pp. [13, 14] occurs another passage which strongly supports the general identification, though it leaves its particular and personal reference still obscure. In this the adepts, who in their mystical Ascent (*miʿrāj*) "attained to that supreme attainment", are said to be "*the Prophets*", who "from thence looked down upon the entire World Invisible [precisely the world of the Heavens]; for he who is in the world of the Realm Supernal is with Allāh, *and hath the keys of the Unseen.* I mean that *from where he is descend the causes of existing things*; for the world of sense *is one of the effects of yonder world of cause*", etc.

This looks almost like a reasoned, philosophic doctrine behind the mystical one, that to Attain to the world of Reality is *ipso facto* to attain to the fount of causation; which involves the ability to direct the Causes which control all the Effects in the Heavens below and the Earth beneath. The Vicegerent does no more than this.

A close scrutiny of these passages leaves one, nevertheless, with the impression that the Adepts whose celestial adventures are there described are too generalized, or perhaps one should say too pluralized, to be identifiable with this single, solitary figure of *al-Muṭā'* as he is presented in our passage. As far as these three passages go, this assumption of the reins of the Universe is only granted to Adepts in their mystic "States", to Prophets in their highly exceptional "Ascent". There is nothing to show that two or more such Attainers might not exist at one time, or that even one must always be existing; in other words, there is no trace of the *complete* and fully developed *Quṭb* doctrine in this treatise. But these considerations make it impossible to identify any one of these Adepts, or all of them together, with the cosmic *Muṭā'*, whose function, related as it is to the very mechanism of the Heavens, is ceaseless, and coextensive with Time itself. And these last four words suggest a further consideration which in itself seems fatal to the proposed identification; namely, that *al-Muṭā'* was Vicegerent *from the very foundation of the world*; he is the one "who commanded the Heavens to be moved" (p. [55, 1. 12]). No Hallāj, no Adept, no *Quṭb*, no Prophet even, ever claimed, or had claimed for him, such priority as this,[1] or even priority at all. But if not, none of them — and, if so, no terrestrial being at all — can claim to fill the rôle of this Vicegerent. The three passages were probably intended only to assert and account for the *karāmāt* of the Saints in their wonder-working, which was parallel to that of the Koranic Jesus.

[1] The question of the priority claimed by a certain school for *Mohammed*, and of the *nūr Muḥammadī*, will be considered later.

The a-priori question of our author's attitude to the *Quṭb* doctrine — whether, consistently with his published writings, he *could* have sustained such a doctrine in this work — is one which can only be indicated here. Professors R. Nicholson and D. B. Macdonald have both communicated to the writer, in reference to the passage under discussion, their opinion that there is an a-priori *im*possibility. To al-Ghazzālī the doctrine was tainted with Imāmism, his special *bête noire* (see his attack on the Taʿlīmites in his *Munqidh*);[1] that since an omnipotent Administrator must also be an infallible Guide (whom Ghazzālī would not have at any price), there is no room for the former in Ghazzālī's thought (thus Professor Macdonald). If the *Muṭāʿ* is not Mohammed, he is certainly no Saint (thus Professor Nicholson).

Be this as it may, the above considerations, drawn from the study of the text itself, and from the passages which prima-facie seemed to point to the *Quṭb-Muṭāʿ* identification, seem finally, when more closely examined, to rule that identification out.

VII. ANOTHER SOLUTION

But there are other passages in our treatise which, when carefully studied, lead to the belief that in Ghazzālī's own mind — though the identification is nowhere explicitly stated or even significantly hinted at — the *Muṭāʿ* is none other than *al-Rūḥ*, THE SPIRIT OF ALLAH.[2]

In S. 17, 87, Mohammed himself had left this enigmatic entity as a divinely uncommunicated, and therefore incommunicable, mystery. The passage runs as follows: "They ask thee of The Spirit: say, The Spirit pertains *to my Lord's Word-of-Command*, and ye have not been communicated knowledge [of It] save a little". The

[1] See Nicholson, *The Idea of Personality in Ṣūfism*, p. 46.
[2] Nicholson, *The Idea of Personality in Ṣūfism*, pp. 44, 45. The identification had occurred independently to the present writer before the appearance of Professor Nicholson's work. It had also occurred independently to Professor D. B. Macdonald.

Arabic of the words italicized is *min amri rabbī*; and we are again faced, at the outset, with the troublesome double meaning of the word *amr*. The phrase *mir amr* might merely mean — perhaps *did* only mean — "a *matter* of"[1] (my Lord's), a vague phrase, common in Arabic, meaning "something that pertains to" so-and-so. But in a case like this, we are not concerned with what Mohammed may originally have meant, but what mystic writers have taken him to mean. And enormously though this verse attracted, puzzled, and baffled commentators and mystics of all ages, the latter seem to have taken the word *amr*, with practical unanimity, in the far more significant sense of "Command". The Hebrew root means "speak", and this meaning is implicit in the Arabic root also, which signifies *spoken* command. And just as later Jewish writers made out of a derivative of this root a Logos Doctrine (*Memra*), so the Mohammedan mystics came near to making a Logos doctrine out of the word *amr*, taking their start from this very text.

A mystery having been definitely started by this text, a haze of mystification was thrown over the entire subject of "spirit": over angels as "spirits", over the human "spirit", the prophetic "spirit"; the inter-relation between these, and the relation of all to "the Spirit"; finally *Its* relation to Allāh. In our treatise there is a full measure of this mystification.

"The Spirit" is *ar-Rūḥ*. With this may be absolutely identified *Rūḥ Allāh* "The Spirit of God"; *Rūḥuhu* "His Spirit"; and *al Rūḥu-l Qudus*[2] (or *Rūḥu-l Qudsi*) "The Transcendent Spirit" — all Koranic expressions.

What then are the considerations which suggest that

---

[1] The word *min* is itself tantalizingly ambiguous. It might mean "(derived) from" or "(part) of" or "pertaining to". Under such circumstances one looks round for the vaguest possible phrase to render the preposition.

[2] This is the Arabic for the Christian "The Holy Spirit". But in Arabic as in early Hebrew the word emphasized the idea of separation or transcendence rather than of righteousness or holiness.

we have in this Figure of Mystery the key to the mystery of the Vicegerent? On this supposition there would be no wonder that Ghazzālī left the figure of the latter a mystery, and declined to divulge the secret of it (p. [55]). He *could* not divulge the whole secret, because by the decree of Allāh and the Book, he could not know it himself — "save a little". And there is no wonder he declined to discuss it, considering the interminable complexities and baffling obscurities of the recorded musings of Ṣūfī doctors on the theme.

At the very outset we are struck by the fact that the word *Muṭā'* occurs in the Koran (S. 81, 23), and not only so, but it occurs as an attribute of the mysterious Agent of Revelation, the vision of whom Mohammed saw at the first (S. 53, 5–16). The text 87, 23, is not definitely cited in *Mishkāt*; and in later Islam the commentators, with their arid tameness, made a stereotyped identification of this Figure with the Angel Gabriel. But the Koran gives no warrant for this; and there is nothing in the *Mihskāt* to show that Ghazzālī thus taught. On the contrary, Gabriel is assigned a low place in the angelic hierachy. No one can read those two Koranic passages (in S. 87 and S. 53) without feeling that Mohammed's awful Visitant *on those two occasions* was the One of absolute supreme rank in the heavenlies: not *a* spirit but *the* Spirit. And It was *muṭā'* — "one who is obeyed". Is it not but a very short step from this to al-*Muṭā'*, *The* Obeyed-One?

The identification, however attractive, would nevertheless be precarious if there was not so much in the *Mishkāt* itself that supports this identification.

(1) On p. [15] the ultimate kindling-place of the graded Lights, of which the Prophets occupy the lower and terrestrial ranks and the Angelic Beings the higher and celestial, is the theme of discussion. Both these ranks of beings are compared to "*lights*" and *all* of them are contrasted with the Highest of all, who is compared to "*fire*", from whose flame these graded lights are successively lit, from top to bottom. Who and what is this Highest of all, next to Allāh? He is said to be " 'an Angel

with countenances seventy thousand'. . . . This is he who is contrasted with all the angelic host, in the words: '*On that day whereon* THE SPIRIT *ariseth, and the Angels, rank on rank*'". It is thus explicitly clear that this Being is the highest of all possible beings in heaven or earth next to Allāh; and so, if the Vicegerent of p. [55] is *also* the highest of all, it would seem inevitable to equate them.

(2) In the very next page, p. [16], Ghazzālī schematizes this conception, and, comparing Allāh with the *Sun* (the source of light in the terrestrial system), he compares the highest of the ministrant lights to the *Moon* (all others being reflections, or reflections-of-reflections, of *it*). This "Highest is the one who is nearest to the Ultimate Light: . . . that Nighest to Allāh, he whose rank comes nighest to the Presence Dominical, which is the Fountain-head of all these Lights". This "Nighest" and "Highest" cannot be other than THE SPIRIT spoken of in the preceding page. And on p. [31] — unless Ghazzālī has suddenly changed all the symbols — the Sun is said to be the Sovereign, while "the antitype of the Moon will be that Sovereign's *Minister* (*wakīl*), for it is through the moon that the sun sheds his light on the world in its own absence, and even so it is through his own *wakīl* that the Sovereign makes his influence felt by subjects who never beheld the royal person". Does not this *wakīl* who stands "highest and nighest" to his Liege-Lord, and who makes himself obeyed by all that Lord's subjects, strongly suggest "the Obeyed One", *al-Muṭāʿ*, the Vicegerent of the conclusion, whose function is, precisely, this?

(3) But what perhaps clinches the matter is the tell-tale word *amr* in that passage about *al-Muṭāʿ* himself on p. [55]. Those who stopped short of complete illumination, he says, identified *al-Muṭāʿ* with Allāh just *because* he moves the *primum mobile* (and so all things) "with his Word of Command" (*amr*). "The explication of which *amr* (he continues), and what it really is, contains much that is obscure, and too difficult for most minds, besides going beyond the scope of this book". And then he says that the *perfect* Illuminati perceived that *al-Muṭāʿ*, the

Obeyed One, is not more than the Highest-other-than-Absolute-Deity, and is related to Him as the sun to Essential Light (mysterious enough this!) or as a glowing coal to the Elemental Fire: and therefore they turned their faces from that Being "who commanded (*amara*) the moving of the Heavens" to the One Existent, Transcendent, Incomparable, Predicateless.

With this word *amr* thus impressed on us with such penetrating significance we turn back to the Koran text: "The *Spirit* pertains to my Lord's *Word of Command* (*amr*) . . ." Unless the word *min* introduces a quite upsetting element, the identification between this SPIRIT and the Commander who is Obeyed seems complete.

But the history of the Ṣūfī teaching on the text shows that *min* need introduce no such upsetting element, and that the practical identification of *Amr* with *Rūḥ*, of The Word of Command with The Spirit, was with the Mystics a familiar idea. It was the explicit teaching of al-Ḥallāj[1]; and the typical "word of command" which this Divine Spirit gave was the fiat "*Kun!*" "Be!"[2] We have seen the fascination which this treatise shows al-Ḥallāj had for al-Ghazzālī. Does it not seem likely, nay almost certain, that in his meditations on the inscrutable text he followed al-Ḥallāj in this equation, with whatever mental reserve regarding the Spirit itself — whether divine or creaturely, eternal or originate? Not that it was only Imāmites or extreme Ṣūfī Sunnites like al-Ḥallāj who asserted the divinity of The Spirit. The ultra-orthodox Ḥanbalites "admitted in some manner the eternity of the *Rūḥ Allāh*".[3] Ibn Ḥanbal himself had given them the lead with a characteristic hedging aphorism (with reminds us

---

[1] Massignon, op. cit., pp. 519–21.

[2] This mediation of the creative function would carry with it the mediation of the administrative. In this connexion use would unquestionably be made of S. 7, 53, "the sun, the moon, and the stars are compelled-to-work by His *amr*" — His Word-of-Command His Spirit — exactly the function of *al-Muṭāʿ*.

[3] Massignon, op. cit., p. 664.

of similar remarks on the *Ṣifāt*, the *Kalām Allāh*, and the Qur'ān), "Whoever says that *al-Rūḥ* is created (*makhlūq*) is a heretic: whoever says that It is eternal (*qadīm*) is an infidel",[1] His followers held fast on to "*uncreate*", and it was hard to keep "*eternal*" from following. No wonder al-Ghazzālī gave a unique and mysterious tinge to his similitude for "The Obeyed", and that It figures, virtually, as an Arian Logos. The more one reflects on what is said about the function of this Being in M., p. [55], and especially Its comparison with the Sun (Allāh being Essential Light), or with glowing coal (Allāh being Elemental Fire), the more unique It appears, and the more mysterious our author's thought about It becomes. For *such* functions, and *such* a relation to Absolute Deity, are in very truth entirely unique, in kind as well as degree; and, thus described, the Vicegerent becomes, in a secondary way, as unique a Figure as is Deity Itself. No wonder the passage raised doubts as to the soundness of our author's monotheism! No wonder he was not anxious to go more deeply into the matter, out of consideration for the limited spiritual capacities of his readers! Perhaps, to preserve his own faith in the Unity, Indivisibility, and absolute Uniqueness of Allāh, he was glad to leave the dark problem of the Vicegerent where Allāh Himself had left that of the Spirit — an uncommunicated and incommunicable mystery, which now he only knew in part, and only saw as in a glass, darkly.

—   —   —   —   —

It remains to consider whether there is any evidence that Ghazzālī extended the equation $Muṭā' = Amr = Rūḥ$ to include the *Nūr Muḥammadī* (as suggested tentatively by Professor R. Nicholson in his lectures on "The Idea of Personality in Sūfism"[2]), the archetypal spirit of Mohammed, the Heavenly Man created in the image of

[1] Ib., p. 661,
[2] Pp. 46, 47, and Lecture III.

God, and regarded as a Cosmic Power on whom depends the order and preservation of the universe. If this could be sustained it would to some extent modify the conclusion reached before that *al-Muṭā'* had nothing to do with any human being, idealized or not, whether a Prophet or even Mohammed; though even so, there would be a vast difference between this archetypal Spirit and the historical Prophet.

While the germs of this idea, as of every other one, may be found much earlier than Ghazzālī's century (the fifth), the study of the sketch which M. Massignon gives of the history of the doctrine (*Hallāj*), pp. 830 seqq.) does not create the impression that it was developed or received in orthodox circles[1] up to Ghazzālī's time. Professor Nicholson does not find it in an orthodox Ṣūfī writer earlier than 'Abdu-l Qādir al-Jīlānī (b. 471, d. 561), in the generation immediately succeeding that of Ghazzālī.[2] After which the doctrine developed and spread amazingly, reaching its height with Ibn al-'Arabī al-Jīlī several centuries later.[3]

Thus the a-priori evidence is this time decidedly against Ghazzālī's having anything to do with this doctrine. Unless, therefore, very clear actual evidence were found in his writings, it would be surely justifiable to assert definitely that it is not Ghazzālīan. It appears *not* to be found in his works other than *al-Mishkāt*. If this is so, it may be further asserted with confidence that it is not found in *al-Mishkāt* either. On the contrary, there is much there that shows a relatively simple, primeval conception of Mohammed on the part of Ghazzālī. For him the archetypal man is Adam, as in the Koran, not

---

[1] It was at first prevalently Imāmite and Shī'ite (Nicholson, *Idea of Personality in Ṣūfism*, p. 58).

[2] He described Muḥammad as *al-rūḥ, al-qudus* and *rūḥ jasad al-wajūd* "the Transcendent Spirit, the Spirit of the body of the Universe".

[3] Nicholson, op. cit., p. 59.

Mohammed.[1] An examination of the passage[2] in which the idea of the "Khalīfa" appears shows that here also his thought was not esoteric, and that Mohammed was not in his mind: he is thinking of the whole human race, or of Adam himself, the first and representative human being, the only "Khalīfa" particularized by the Koran. And the one passage in the *Mishkāt* which at first sight does look as if it contained a "high doctrine of the person" of Mohammed, turns out on closer inspection to prove the exact reverse, viz. that essentially he belonged to this world and to the time-order — to the prophets, *above* whom are ranked the celestial "Lights" culminating, as we have seen, in the Supreme Angelical, The Spirit. This passage is on pp. [14, 15]. Here we have the Transcendent Spirit Prophetical (*al-Rūḥ al-qudus al-nabawī*) attributed to Mohammed as prophet, by reason of which he is called a Luminous Lamp (*sirāj munīr*). If this stood by itself we might be suspicious of something esoteric. But immediately after this the other prophets, and even saints, are said to be "Lamps", and to possess, as Its name implies, this Spirit Prophetical. The sequel shows that this Spirit is the Fire from which all the Angelical lights above and the Prophetical lights beneath are lit, and that this Spirit is the Supreme Angelical, "The Spirit", as in the passage already discussed.[3]

To sum up the conclusion to which I have been lead by a consideration of the evidence of the *Mishkāt* itself, together with the a-priori evidence which supplements it and is checked by it — the heavenly Vicegerent is the Spirit of Allāh, the Transcendent Spirit of Prophecy, the divine Word-of-Command; he is not a *Quṭb* or any

---

[1] M., p. [34].

[2] M., p. [22].

[3] See above, pp. 82, 83. The only thing that puzzles is that Ghazzālī sometimes distributes and pluralizes this Spirit, see p. [15, 1. 4], and p. [22, 1. 8]. In each case the regulative singular, however, is close by. This reminds one of Rev. iv, 5 and v, 6, compared with Rev. ii, 7.

Adept; he is not Mohammed nor the archetypal spirit of Mohammed.

Whether this mystery of the Vicegerent was connected in our author's mind with that of the divine-human, archetypal *Ṣūra*, as developed by al-Ḥallāj and other advanced Mystics, will be discussed later.

VIII. AL-GHAZZALI AND THE SEVEN SPHERES

The Seven Planetary Heavens played a great part in Platonic,[1] Neoplatonic, and Gnostic-theosophical schemes. The naive adoption by Mohammed (in the Koran) of the Ptolemaic celestial construction was one of the things which added picturesqueness to early Mohammedan tradition and theology; caused endless trouble to generations of later theologians; made it easier for Neoplatonic ideas to graft themselves on to Islam; gave to the raptures of the Mystics sensuous form and greater definition; and afforded to the Philosophers a line of defence, and even of attack, in their war with the Theologians.[2] And the allusions of the Koran were heavily reinforced by the legend of the *Mi'rāj*, the exact origin of which is obscure, but which appears in a highly developed form almost from the first. The influence of the *Mi'rāj* is indeed evident in page after page of the *Mishkāt*.

Al-Ghazzālī's sympathies in regard to this subject were divided. He disliked the Philosophers, and this made him displeased with their confident assertions about the Heavens, while he detested the "philosophical" profit to which they put them. On the other hand, he was a Ṣūfī, and thus in closest touch with persons who made very similar assertions about the Heavens, and also put them to profit in their own way. Finally, he was an Ash'arite Theologian, belonging to a school which had recently, after much trouble,

---

[1] See the *Vision of Er* in *The Republic*, bk. x.

[2] See Averroes' *Kitāb al Kashf an manāhij al adillā*, quoted above on p. 68, note 2.

eliminated from theology the dangerous ideas to which Mohammed's naive attitude to the Heavens had given rise.

This uncertainty of touch comes out, as might be expected, in a treatise like *al-Mishkāt* with its blend of scholasticism and Neoplatonically-tinctured mysticism. The Heavens figure continually in its pages. They seem to play a most important part both in thought and in experience — towards the close of the book a *determining* part. Yet it is impossible to make out exactly what that part was, in the mind of al-Ghazzālī himself.

On p. [23] we have a correlation of the human microcosm and the macrocosm of the celestial realm, Ptolemaically construed, in describing the Ascension of a God-united soul. The adept's body-and-soul structure is conceived of as subsisting in three planes or Spheres, which are correlated with the three lower spheres of the Seven Planetary Heavens. From the highest of these (the Intelligence) the soul takes its departure and ascends through the four upper Heavens (*ila saba'i ṭabaqāt*) to the Throne [beyond the outermost Heaven]. Thus he "fills all things" by his upward Ascent just as Allāh did by His downward Descent (*nuzūl*). In all this the pronoun "he" stands for the soul *who is now Allāh-possessed and united*, as described in what immediately precedes. It is the upward ascent of *Allāh* (corresponding to His *nuzūl ila-l samā' i-l dunyā*), and not of the Adept only.

On the other hand, in p. [29], this Ascent is described in purely psychological terms, without this schema of the Heavens. and on p. [13] we have the following: "Do not imagine that I mean by the World Supernal the World of the [Seven] Heavens, though they are 'above' in respect of part of our world of sense-perception. *These* Heavens are equally present to our apprehension and that of the lower animals. But a man finds the doors of the Realm Celestial closed to him, neither does he become of or belonging to that Realm (*malakūtī*), unless this earth to him 'be changed into that which is not earth; and

89

likewise the heavens';[1] . . . and his 'heaven' come to be all
that transcends his sense. This is the first Ascension for
every Pilgrim who has set out on his Progress to the
nearness of the Presence Dominical". And he continues:
"The Angels . . . are part of the World of the Realm
Celestial, floating ever in the Presence of the Transcendence, whence they gaze down upon our world inferior".

The last lines hardly give us the same ultra-
spiritualizing impression which is conveyed by their
predecessors. And, as we have already seen (Introduction, pp. 7–10), the part played by the Spheres with
their Angels in the last section of the book is decisive, and
there does not seem to be *there* any spiritualizing
whatever.

How far, therefore, these passages are mere word-play,
pious picturesqueness, or how far they represent speculation of a rather far-reaching character, is one of the
puzzles of the book. In the *Tahāfut*, demolishing the
arrogant claim of the Philosophers to *prove* their doctrine
of the Spheres by syllogistic demonstration (*burhān*), he
said: "The secrets of The Kingdom are not to be scanned
by means of such fantastic imaginations as these; Allāh
gives none but His Prophets and Saints (*anbiyā'* and
awliyā') to scan them, and that by inspiration, not by
demonstration".[2] So then there *were* mysteries and
secrets in regard to the Spheres. In the *Mishkāt* we are
able to see pretty clearly that Ghazzālī had his; but we
are not able to see just what they were. He has kept *this*
secret well.

IX. Anthropomorphism and Theomorphism in
al-Mishkat

The doctrine of *mukhālafa* — that the divine essence
and characteristics wholly and entirely "differ from" the

[1] S. 14, 48.

[2] Tah., p. 60. Quoted in the writer's article in *Der Islām*, see pp.
134–6, 151, 152, where parts of the subject are gone into in greater
detail.

human — appears to be asserted, as this treatise's *last* word, in its most extreme and intransigent form. For the conclusion of the whole matter, the end of the quest for truth for those who "Arrive", is "an Existent who transcends ALL that is comprehensible by human Insight . . . transcendent of and separate from every characterization that in the foregoing we have made".[1]

Nevertheless, the *Mishkāt* itself seems to be one long attempt to modify or even negate this its own bankrupt conclusion. Indeed, it goes unusual lengths in asserting a certain ineffable *likeness* between Allāh and man. It is true that the usual anthropomorphic expressions — the Hand, the Session on the Throne, the Descent to the Lowest Sphere, etc., those perennial sources for Mohammedan theologizing — are used and are discounted in the usual way. But they are, in reality, only discounted by being replaced by a Ṣūfī system of theomorphism. This has three main aspects —

    (1) a quasi-Platonic doctrine of terrestrial type and celestial antitype;

    (2) the relation of the divine and human *rūḥ* (spirit);

    (3) the relation of the divine and human *ṣūra* ("image", "form").

    (1) The whole of the first two parts of the treatise are practically an exposition of an Islamico-Platonic

[1] In Ghazzālī the most extreme Agnosticism and the most extreme Gnosticism meet, and meet at this point; for, as he says (p. [25]), "things that go beyond one extreme pass over to the extreme opposite". For him "Creed because Incredible" becomes "Gnosis because Agnoston". What saved the *Universe* for him from his nihilistic theologizing was his ontology (see below, pp. 61 seqq.). What saved *God* for him from his obliterating agnosticism was the experience of the mystic leap, his own personal *mi'rāj*. This may have been non-rational, but it was to him experience. Even those who regard the sensational experiences of Ṣūfism as having been pure self-hypnotism cannot condemn them, and the sense of reality they brought, in relation to the man who had thought his way out of both atheism and pantheism, and yet would have been left at the end of the quest, by his thinking alone, with an Unknown and Unknowable Absolute.

typology. It is not explicitly said that earthly things are more or less faint copies of "the patterns of things in the heavens", though this is probably implicit in what *is* said, namely, that the heavenly realities (*huqā'iq*), (*ma'ānī*), all have their symbols on earth. These symbols or types, as their Arabic term itself suggests (*amthāl*), do possess a "resemblance" to their celestial antitypes, for, as al-Ghazzālī remarks, "the thing compared (*al-mushabbah*, the antitype) is in some sort parallel, and bears resemblance, to the thing compared therewith (*al-mushabbah bihi*, the type or symbol), whether that resemblance be remote or near; a matter again which is unfathomably deep".[1] Ghazzālī can hardly be allowed to elude the application of this true principle to Allāh Himself, considering that this very Koran-verse which it is the object of the entire treatise to expound begins with a simile. "Light" is the chosen, or rather the God-given symbol, wherewith Allāh is "compared", and which therefore He must "in some sort resemble". This analogy of light floods the whole book. Now Allāh is the Sun: now the Light of lights: and at the end, in the same breath in which Abu Ḥāmid, with the incorrigible inconsistency which so angered Averroes, denied the validity of the similitude, description, relation, or even predication in regard to Allāh, we are told that He stands in relation to His Vicegerent (or "wakeel" in a parallel passage) as the pure *Light*-essence to the sun, or as the Elemental *Fire* to a glowing coal. Theomorphism has "in some sort" been admitted.

(2) In the *Iḥyā' al'Ulūm* Ghazzālī speaks of the human *rūḥ* as *amr rabbānī* "a divine affair" (*amr* must surely bear here its other meaning); and he is there very anxious, not to say agitated, over the esoteric character of the doctrine; it must be kept a dead secret from the Many! it must not be set forth in a book![2] "The specific characteristic which differentiates humanity [from the

[1] M., p. [14].

[2] See *Mīzān*, p. 214, quoted above.

lower creation] is something which it is not lawful to indite in a book".[1] The thing that agitates him is the relation of this human *rūḥ* to the Spirit of God, *rūḥ Allāh*, and Its relation to Allāh. The matter is esoteric — it is to be "grudged" to the "commons" — because it is dangerous ground. It is dangerous ground because one has to talk warily in order to avoid a violation of the uniqueness of Allāh, which would involve confusing Creator with created, and so passing gradually to *ishrāk*, which is the worst "infidelity".

This particular anxiety is not reflected in the present treatise; it is strange that the mystery of *rūḥ* does not figure in the list (see above, p. 3) over which the author's *favete linguis!* is inscribed.[2] He is mainly occupied with working out what the New Testament calls the "operations", rather than the nature, of the spirit. In so doing the singular "spirit" becomes plural "spirits", *arwāḥ*, which, as already observed, happens also in the Book of the Revelation. Ghazzālī works out the theory of the several "spirits" of the human psychology; then the graded "spirits" of the heavenly hosts; and then the Neoplatonic or theosophic idea of the gradation of all these (in *maqāmāt*), and the way in which they are "lit" (*muqtabasa*) from each other in order: we must not say "derived", for that would involve him in the emanationism he was ever anathematizing, yet for ever incurring the suspicion of.[3] In all this his tone is open, easy, confident. The special mystery of *The* Spirit had been already discounted in the Koran, so that was harmless. As for the identification of *Rūḥ-Muṭā‘*, if our theory is correct, *that* was a grand secret. But that secret he never intended even to hint at, and it would really seem as if we had surprised and betrayed a *sirr maknūn*!

---

[1] *Iḥyā*, iv, p. 294, quoted in a letter to the writer from Professor R. Nicholson.

[2] The human *'aql* does figure on that list, pp. [6, 7].

[3] See the writer's op. cit. in *Der Islām*, pp. 138–141.

(3) It was the *ṣūra* tradition,[1] "ALLAH CREATED ADAM AFTER HIS IMAGE", that above all else led Moslem thinkers into temptation — the temptation of trenching on the uniqueness of Allāh. Its very riskiness seems, however, to have fascinated them supremely from the very outset. Not one of them could let it alone. In this very treatise Ghazzālī returns to it again and again. Perhaps it would accord with inner truth to say rather that both he and others returned to that tradition not so much as moths fascinated by a dangerous glare, but as those who are feeling cold return for warmth and cheer to even an alien fire. The aphorism, sacred as a Koran text, was the assertion and pledge that man somehow is, or may become, "like God". The word *ṣūra* became the symbol and the guarantee of theomorphism.

In the first allusion in the *Mishkāt* to this tradition (p. [9]), the point of the similarity is the human intelligence (*'aql*). In virtue of his *intelligence*, Ghazzālī hints, man is "after the image of Allāh". The *'aql* is "Allāh's balance-scale upon earth".[2] In its own sphere it is infallible.[3] From the *'aql*, as from a firm "taking-off" place, souls make their mystic Ascension to the heavenlies.[4] It is because it is thus the specifically human faculty that it is a determinative element in the human *ṣūra*.[5]

The second allusion (M., p. [24]) carries us very much further — even to that verge from which Moslem mystics so often looked dizzily down, but from which they so seldom fell, into the pantheistic abyss. Behold a human soul in completest Union (*jam'*) with Deity, sitting on The Throne, and administering all things in heaven and earth! "Well might one", says our author, "in looking upon such an one", get a new view of this tradition. Is not such a uniate, indeed, "after the image of Allāh"? But, he continues, "after contemplating that word more deeply one becomes aware that it has an interpretation

---

[1] Gen. i. 27, though Islām ignores the parentage.
[2] M., p. [20].   [3] Ib., p. [10].   [4] Ib., p. [24].   [5] Ib., p. [40].

like [al-Ḥallāj's] 'I am the One Real'."[1] Unfortunately he has omitted to indicate what precisely that interpretation is. We have a tantalizing author to deal with.

What was that interpretation?

Probably we do not find it in the third passage (pp. [34, 35]), though it is deeply influenced by Ḥallājian thought. There is in the celestial world something which "développe, modalise, et concerte entre elles les créations divines . . . une certaine structure interne particulière à l'acte créateur".[2] This living order, this organized "Presence" (ḥaḍar), is symbolized by the word *Image*, or *Form*. And this macrocosmic ḥaḍra has its earthly counterpart in an analogous *human* form, or ṣūra, which has the same "structure interne particulière" (it is alluded to on p. [22, 1. 1], and p. [34, 1. 3], and described in detail on pp. [39–41]). Therefore, man, formed in this Form, is "after the Form, the Image, of this Merciful One (al Raḥmān)". Ghazzālī's explanation of his preference for this variation of the tradition, to which, however, he by no means always adheres, is difficult to follow. But the general idea clearly is that "but for this 'mercy' [i.e. of these two correlative and coincident Forms] every son of Adam would have been powerless to know his Lord, for 'only he who knows himself knows his Lord'". The wheel has, indeed, brought us round a strange circle! Through the eternal grace of theomorphism we win back to a higher anthropomorphism, so that the proper study of God is — man! And this from the writer whose last word is that Allāh must not have so

[1] How translate this "*Ana-l Ḥaqq*"? Not by Jesus' "*I am the Truth*", tempting though this is. "*I am the Absolute*" would be a parallel rendering in modern philosophic parlance. Professor Nicholson's "*I am God*" is startling, but illuminating because perfectly justifiable; for al-Ḥaqq and Allāh are mutually and exclusively convertible.

[2] Massignon, op. cit., p. 519, describing Ḥallāj's doctrine of the divine rūḥ, and exactly hitting off Ghazzālī's difficult thought on p. [24, II, 2, 3] (cf. p. [22, 1. 2]). But from this point of view rūḥ and ṣūra merge into each other, as a careful comparison of the two *Mishkāt* passages just cited shows.

much as an attribute predicated of Him, or the divine uniqueness will be violated! Truly, thus the whirligig of
thought brings in his revenges.

We have already seen many indications that before he
wrote this treatise Ghazzālī must have been deep in the
study of al-Ḥallāj; and the passage we have just been
considering may be added to these indications. Yet there
is no overt trace in it, or elsewhere in the *Mishkāt*, of al-
Ḥallāj's profoundest thought on this matter of the
Divine-Adamic; no trace of that strange Figure — that
Epiphany of humanized Deity, or Apotheosis of ideal-
Humanity — which was presented by Allāh to the angels
for worship or ever the first man was created, and in
which He Himself, on behalf of the human race, swore
unto Himself the Covenant (*m-thāq*) of allegiance. For
this conception, which has the closest interrelations with
all the moments of the above discussion — *rūḥ, amr, ṣūra,
nūr-Muḥammadī* — the reader must be referred to the
grand work which has brought to light so many hidden
things, M. Louis Massignon's *La Passion d' Al Ḥosayn-ibn-
Manṣour al-Ḥallāj.*[1] Ghazzālī's silence on this so
remarkable development of the *Ṣūra* tradition would
suggest that it was precisely here that he felt it dangerous
to follow al-Ḥallāj. What was possible for the seer might
send the theologian over the line where Islām ends and
pantheism begins. On the other hand, is it possible that
here we have the explanation of our author's em-
barrassed words on p. [55] "on account of a Mystery
which it is not in the competence of this book to reveal"?
His inmost thought may have been, "Perhaps al-Ḥallāj
has penetrated here to something of what the Koran itself
[in the Spirit-Verse] left obscure. I neither assert, nor
deny. *Allāhu a'lam!* "

[1] Pp. 485, 599–602. In a note Massignon hazards the tentative
suggestion that this epiphanized God (called by al-Ḥallāj *al-Nāsūt* in
contra-distinction from the unknowable *al-Lāhūt*) is analogical to, or
suggestive of Ghazzālī's *Vicegerent* (p. 601, n. 5). The suggestion is
thrilling, as we see. It must be repeated that there is no overt trace of
the doctrine in M.

Thus we come to the ultimate question — the ultimate question with every Ṣūfī writer and book — does he and it escape pantheism? What light comes from this "Niche for Lights" upon this obscure question?

X. PANTHEISM AND AL-GHAZZALI, IN AL-MISHKAT

The root question in regard to al-Ghazzālī, and every other advanced mystic and adept in Islām, is the question of Pantheism: did he succeed in balancing himself upon the edge of the pantheistic abyss, and finding some foothold for his creationist theism, some position that cleared his conscience towards his orthodox co-religionists? Or did he fail in this? The *Miskhāt* contains a good deal that is relevant to this final issue.

It contains much, in the first place, which on the face of it reads like naked pantheism; and in particular the whole passage on pp. [19, 20] and [22–4], where not only is the most extreme language of the extreme wing of Ṣūfism (*Ana-l Ḥaqq*[1] and the rest) quoted with guarded approval, but there is open eulogy of the formula *lā huwa illā Huwa* "there is no it but HE", which is declared to be more expressive of real, absolute truth than the Mohammedan creed itself *lā ilāha ill-Allāh* "there is no god but God". This would seem to be as unreserved an assertion of flat pantheism as could be found in philosophic Hinduism itself. Equally worthy of philosophic Hinduism is Ghazzālī's "*He is everything*: He is that He is: none but He has ipseity or heity at all . . ." (p. [22]). And then again the experience of the advanced Initiates and Adepts is described in terms of thorough pantheism: to them "the plurality of things fell away in its entirety. They were drowned in the absolute Unitude, and their intelligences were lost in its abyss" (p. [19]); and when they return to earthly illusions again from that world of reality they "confess with one voice that they had seen *nought existent* there save the One Real (Allāh)". *Existent*! Do words mean what they say?

[1] Which, it must be remembered, might not unfairly be translated "I am God"; see footnote above.

No, not precisely! with a Ghazzālī, and with Mohammedan mystics, clinging desperately to orthodoxy! The matter, in fact, turns precisely on this word "existent". What *is* existence? What *is* non-existence? It was Ghazzālī's ontological philosophy that seems to have yielded him a fulcrum on which he could precariously balance the pantheistic and the deistic moments of his religious thought.

This philosophy is poetically stated in our treatise, but in spite of the poetic, imaginative diction it can be recognized as identical with his usual doctrine.[1] It will be found on pp. [17–19, 21, 22]. We have there a picturesque representation of a doctrine well known to the schoolmen of Islām, that Not-Being is a sort of dark limbo in which the Contingent awaits the creative word *Kun* "Be!" — compared in this "Light"-treatise to a ray of light from the One Self-existing Being. Neither the Greeks nor the schoolmen could ever quite get over the feeling that, in predicating anything of Not-being or a Nonentity, in using the word "is" in a sentence with Not-being or a Nonentity as its subject, you have in some way ascribed, not existence, but a sort of quasi-being, to that subject. Hegel's solution was so to evacuate the category of mere, bare "Being" of all content, and to demonstrate its consequent total impoverishment and inanity, that it could be seen to be the equivalent of Not-being. This was impossible for the schoolmen, above all for Oriental schoolmen, even of the most contradictory schools, who regarded the category of "pure" being (they would never have said "mere") as the sublimest and most radiant of all the categories, and the very object of the whole quest of life. But the obverse of the Hegelian paradox may nevertheless be seen in their ascription to contingent not-yet-being a sort of quasi-existence. The effect of the creative word was simply to turn this potential into actual being. Thus the universe, always contingent,

[1] See, for example, *Munqidh* and the Lesser *Madnūn* (if that is Ghazzālī's).

indeed, but formerly potential-contingent, *now* became actual-contingent.

All this is schematized in *al-Mishkāt*. The limbo becomes Darkness (p. 30); the potential-contingent, Dark Things[1]; the divine creator, the Sun; the creative act, a Ray from His real being, whereby a dark Nonentity flashes into being and becomes an Entity, but an Entity that depends continuously on the permanent illumination of that ray, for in the Mohammedan creational scheme, at any rate, Creator is equally capable of being Annihilator.

At this point Ghazzālī's tortured thought is greatly helped out by the ambiguous word *wajh*, which has two senses, or rather three. Face, Side, Aspect (logical). This gave him a formula: it was not the first time, nor the last, that the ambiguity of the chief word in a theological formula has been welcome to all concerned. He could take the Koran texts *"the Wajh of everything faces (muwai-jah) to Him and is turned in His direction"*, and *"Whithersoever*

---

[1] It is just here that, as it seems to the writer, the Philosophers with their Aristotelian doctrine of the eternity — the formless substrate of things — might well have forced a place for *their* thought, in spite of the Ghazzālīan wrath against them and it. For when the dark "self-aspect" of these contingencies of the Theologians is considered, prior to their "existence" (p. [59]), is there much to choose between the eternal potentiality asserted of them by Ghazzālī, and the eternity asserted for *hyle* by the Philosophers? Ghazzālī himself quotes a saying of Mohammed (p. [13]), on to which these Philosophers would eagerly have seized as proving their point: "Allāh created the creation in darkness, then sent an effusion of His light upon it". For a man who was using this divine light-emanation to typify the act of creation, of calling out of not-being to being, it was dangerous surely to give, apparently, so powerful an indication as this of a previous *creation* in "darkness" (= not-being in Ghazzālī's chosen symbology). It might very well have been claimed by the Philosophers that this creation-in-darkness is precisely their formless, chaotic *hyle*, eternal as darkness is eternal before the light shines. The Philosophers *did* pretend to prove their thesis from the Koran; see Averroes' *Manāhij*, ed. Müller, p. 13 (=Cairo ed. *Falsafat Ibn Rushd*, p. 12), where the following texts are cited in support, S. 11, 9; 14, 49; 41, 10.

they turn themselves, there is the Wajh of Allāh"; and the *ḥadīth qudṣī, "Everything is a perishing thing except His Wajh"*; and could then play on the word. In ancient and mediaeval times the merest plays on words were not considered figures of speech but profundities of thought. Quibbles masqueraded as discoveries. And so this word (*a*) enabled Ghazzālī to keep his hold on creationism on the one hand, for *these* were "things" sure enough, all turned towards the central Sun and dependent for their existence on its creative light; and there was also the sound logical position, that under this aspect (*wajh*) of *relatedness* these things have actual being (p. [18]). So the actuality of the universe is saved, and the abyss of pantheism is avoided. *And* (*b*), on the other hand, he could say to the pantheistic Ṣūfī (and to himself in that mood), that equally under this "aspect" of relatedness things, if and when considered *an sich*, had no existence, were not existent at all. The only Existent was the *Wajh Allāh* (p. [22]), that is, Allāh Himself, for, as he carefully informs us (p. [19]), Allāh cannot possibly be said to be "greater" (*akbar*) than His own *wajh*; and must, therefore, be identical therewith. And thus the out-and-out pantheist might well feel his case complete; the last vestige of dualism disappears; Allāh is All, and All is Allāh, *lā mawjūda ill-Allāh* (M. p. [18])! As Ghazzālī himself put it, Allāh is the Sun and besides the sun there is only the sun's light. *Quid plura?*

Nevertheless, it may be believed that Ghazzālī himself contrived to use this ontology so as to *keep*, not lose, his hold on the reality[1] and actuality of things, and that early training, central theological orthodoxy, and strong common-sense proved by its help too strong for the pull towards pantheism, with which his late Ṣūfism with its Neoplatonic atmosphere and sensational ecstasies un-

---

[1] I.e. in the modern or western sense of the word, = "objectivity". To the mediaeval eastern thinker the Arabic word meant rather "ideality". It is a case of the difference between phenomenal and transcendental reality.

doubtedly did pull him — as Ṣūfism pulled every Mohammedan mystical devotee. Is it not notable that even in the lyrical passages in this treatise, in which he describes (with a rather scared unction) the Mystics' intoxication and the verbal blasphemies which that state so happily permitted, and which were permitted to that state, Ghazzālī keeps his head, and preserves the same cautious balance as he does in the ontological sections (see pp. [19, 20])? When these inebriates, he says, became sober again, "and they came under the sway of the intelligence . . . they knew that that had not been actual *Identity*, but only something resembling Identity" (not *homoousion* but *homoiousion*!). If we correctly translate *ittuḥād*[1] thus, the remark is of crucial importance; for the ultimate test of a complete Pantheism is whether things are *identical* with God, or only *united* with Him. All classes of mystics without exception assert at least the latter — it is the "Union" of the Christian, as of the Muslim, Catholic; but only those who have actually surrendered their balance and toppled over into the pantheistic abyss assert the former. And Ghazzālī did not do so. He goes on to quote yet another "drunken" cry of a soul in Union, "I am He whom I love, and He whom I love is I", and shows how even here a distinction is preserved. And then that other, who likened the Union to a transparent Glass filled with red Wine —

"The glass is thin, the wine is clear.
The twain are alike, the matter is perplexed:
For 'tis as though there were wine and no wine-glass
there,
Or as though there were wine-glass and nought of wine".

And thus comments: "Here there is a difference between saying 'The wine *is* the wine-glass' and ''tis *as though it were* the wine-glass'." The former, he tells us, is *Identity* (*ittiḥād*), the latter *Unification* (*tawḥīd*), not in the com-

---

[1] Professor Macdonald prefers "identification", to bring out the verb-aspect of the *maṣdar* more clearly.

monalty's meaning of *tawḥīd*, he honestly says (p. [20]), for *them* this is one of "the mysteries which we are not at liberty to discuss" — but at the same time not inconsistent with that meaning. What he had in mind was, perhaps, something like this: "I reject the herd's interpretation of *tawḥīd*, the mere declaration-of-the-oneness of Allāh, as a bare truism, miserable in its inadequacy. I likewise reject the other extreme, the pantheist's interpretation of the word as an absolute denial of the actuality of things, or an assertion that things are Allāh. Against them both I assert that Allāh and the Universe constitute a UNITY, but one wherein the Universe is a wholly relative to and dependent on Allāh, for existence or non-existence; preservation or annihilation. All existing things are and must be 'united' to Allāh. But even this must not be declared openly, for, then, what about Iblīs, Hell, and the Damned? I must not seem to teach 'universalism' any more than pantheism. *Allāhu a'lam!*"

It therefore seems to the writer that Ghazzālī's position, which he tortured rather than explained when he tried to describe and illustrate it, really amounted to nothing more than the inevitable distinction between absolute and relative being; between things when viewed relationally, in their relation to their Author, and things viewed apart from that relation. Neither Author nor Things were to be denied actuality, or reality, as we understand the latter term. As between Allāh and human intelligences he even goes great lengths (in this very treatise of all others) in asserting parallelism and comparability, similarity therefore[1]; *but* between *Allāh* and all else ONE fundamental all-sufficient difference had to be asserted; namely, ALLAH is *self-subsistent, qayyūm*; things are *not* so. This distinction was the minimum one; yet also the maximum, for it preserved at once Creator and created, and gave actuality to each. There is, in truth, a good deal of wilful paradox in the *Mishkāt*, of Oriental

[1] And to assert similarity between two things is at once to have asserted *two*, and a distinction between them. See M., p. [7].

hyperbole, of pious highfalutin,[1] *intended* perhaps to scare the "unco" orthodox of the day, to make their flesh creep a little for their health's sake, and to "wake them out of their dogmatic slumbers". For it is in the *Mishkāt* that we find the following words, too, which seem plain and harmless enough: "Being is itself divided into that which has being-in-itself. The being of this latter is borrowed, having no existence by itself. Nay, if it is regarded in and by itself it is pure not-being. *Whatever being it has* is due to its relation to not-itself, which is not real being at all . . ." In other words, it is by a purely arbitrary mental abstraction that we "regard derived being in and by itself". The impossibility of really *effecting* this abstraction is precisely what preserves to derived being its measure of actuality — "whatever being it has . . ."[2] To *us* these last words are a clear concession of reality to conditioned being. It is true Ghazzālī denies reality to it in the next sentence. But this only shows that when an Oriental talks of "Real" he means what we mean by "Unconditioned", and that when he is thinking of "Conditioned or Relative" he says "Unreal". The matter has become one of terms.

It is impossible to demand more than this from Ghazzālī as philosopher-theologian. He was, perhaps, not more successful than other eastern theologians in finding a place for the universe, philosophically, with or in Allāh. But has western philosophy been any more successful in finding a place for Allāh, philosophically, with or in the universe?

[1] Is not this true for *all* Ṣūfī writers? Do we not take their language too seriously? It parades as scientific; it is really poetico-rhetorical.

[2] Gh. has no more use for the Noumenon, for the *Ding an sich*, than had the post-Kantians; though for how different reasons!

TRANSLATION

[The references in square brackets are to the pages of the Cairo Arabic Edition].

THE NICHE FOR LIGHTS
(*Mishkāt al-Anwār*)

Praise to ALLAH! *who poureth forth light; and giveth sight; and, from His mysteries' height, removes the veils of night!*

And Prayer for MOHAMMED! *of all lights the Light; Sire of them that do the right; Beloved of The Sovereign of Might; Evangelist of the forgiven in His sight; to Him devoted quite; to sinner and to infidel the Arm that knows to fight and smite!*

You have asked me, dear brother — and may Allāh decree for you the quest of man's chiefest bliss, make you candidate for the Ascent to the highest height, anoint your vision with the light of Reality, and purge your inward parts from all that is not the Real! — you have asked me, I say, to communicate to you the mysteries of the Lights Divine, together with the allusions behind the literal meaning of certain texts in the Koran and certain sayings in the Traditions.

And principally this text[1]:

"*Allāh is the Light of the Heavens and of the Earth. The similitude of His Light is as it were a Niche wherein is a Lamp: the Lamp within a Glass: the Glass as it were a pearly Star. From a Tree right blessed is it lit, an Olive-tree neither of the East nor of the West, the Oil whereof were wellnigh luminous though Fire touched it not: Light upon Light!*

"*But as for the Infidels, their deeds are as it were massed Darkness upon some fathomless sea, the which is overwhelmed with billow topped by billow topped by cloud: Darkness on Darkness piled! so that when a man putteth forth his hand he well-nigh can see it not. Yea, the man for whom Allāh doth not cause light, no light at all hath he*".

---

[1] The Light-Verse in S. 24, 35. The Darkness-Verse, which almost immediately follows, and is mentioned in the exposition, has been added.

What is the significance of His comparison of LIGHT with Niche, and Glass, and Lamp, and Oil, and Tree?

And this Tradition:

"Allāh hath Seventy Thousand Veils of Light and Darkness: were He to withdraw their curtain, then would the splendours of His Aspect[1] surely consume everyone who apprehended Him with his sight".

Such is your request. But in making it you have assayed to climb an arduous ascent, so high that the height thereof cannot be so much as gauged by mortal eyes [3]. You have knocked at a locked door which is only opened to those who know and *"are established in knowledge"*.[2] Moreover, not every mystery is to be laid bare or made plain, but —

"Noble hearts seal mysteries like the tomb".

Or, as one of those who Know has said —

"To divulge the secret of the Godhead is to deny God".

Or, as the prophet has said —

"There is a knowledge like the form of a hidden thing, known to none save those who know God".

If then these speak of that secret, only the Children of Ignorance will contradict them. And howsoever many these Ignorants be, the Mysteries must from the gaze of sinners be kept inviolate.

But I believe that your heart has been opened by the Light and your consciousness purged of the darkness of Ignorance. I will, therefore, not be so niggardly as to deny you direction to these glorious truths in all their fineness and all their divineness; for the wrong done in keeping Wisdom from her Children is not less than that of yielding her to those who are Strangers to her. As the poet hath it —

"He who bestoweth Knowledge on fools loseth it,
And he who keepeth the deserving from her doeth a wrong".

You must, however, be content with a very summarized explanation of the subject; for the full

[1] Or Countenance; see Introduction, p. 99.
[2] Cf. S. 6.

demonstration of my theme would demand a treatment of both its principles and its parts for which my time is at present insufficient, and for which neither my mind nor my energies are free. The keys of all hearts are in the hands of Allāh: He opens them when He pleases, as He pleases, and with what He pleases. At this time, then it shall suffice to open up to you three chapters or parts, whereof the first is as hereunder follows.

PART I. — LIGHT, AND LIGHTS: PRELIMINARY STUDIES

1. "Light" as Physical Light; as the Eye; as the Intelligence

The Real Light is Allāh; and the name "light" is otherwise only predicated metaphorically and conveys no real meaning.

To explain this theme: you must know that the word light is employed with a three-fold signification: the first [4] by the Many, the second by the Few, the third by the Fewest of the Few. Then you must know the various grades of light that relate to the two latter classes, and the degrees of reality appertaining to these grades, in order that it may be disclosed to you, as these grades become clear, that ALLAH is the highest and the ultimate Light: and further, ·as the reality appertaining to each grade is revealed, that Allāh *alone* is the Real, the True Light, and beside Him there is no light at all.

Take now the first signification. Here the word light indicates a *phenomenon*. Now a phenomenon, or appearance, is a relative term, for a thing necessarily appears to, or is concealed from, something other than itself; and thus its appearance and its non-appearance are both relative. Further, its appearance and its non-appearance are relative to *perceptive faculties*; and of these the most powerful and the most conspicuous, in the opinion of the Many, are the *senses*, one of which is the sense of *sight*. Further, things in relation to this sense of sight fall under these categories: (1) that which by itself is not visible, as dark bodies; (2) that which is by itself visible, but cannot make visible anything else, such as luminaries like the stars, and fire before it blazes up; (3) that which is by itself visible, and also makes visible, like the sun and the moon, and fire when it blazes up, and lamps. Now it is in regard to this third category that the name "light" is given: sometimes to that which is effused from these luminaries and falls on the exterior of opaque bodies, as when we say "The earth is lighted up", or "The light of the sun falls on the earth", or "The lamplight falls on wall or on garment"; and sometimes to the luminaries themselves, because they are self-luminous. In sum, then, light is an expression for that which *is by itself visible and* [5] *makes other things visible*, like the sun. This is the definition of, and the reality concerning, light, according to its first signification.

We have seen that the very essence of light is appearance to a percipient; and that perception depends on the existence of two things — light and a seeing eye. For, though light is that which appears and causes-to-appear, it neither appears nor causes-to-appear to the blind. Thus percipient spirit is as important as perceptible light *quā* necessary element of perception; nay, 'tis the more important, in that it is the percipient spirit which apprehends, and through which apprehension takes place; whereas light is not apprehensive, neither does apprehension take place through it, but merely when it is present. By the word light, in fact, is more properly understood that visualizing light which we call the eye. Thus men apply the word light to the light of the eye, and say of the weak-sighted that *"the light of his eye* is weak", and of the blear-eyed that *"the light of his vision* is impaired", and of the blind that *"his light* is quenched". Similarly of the pupil of the eye it is said that it concentrates "the light" of vision, and strengthens it, the eye-lashes being given by the divine wisdom a black colour, and made to compass the eye every way round about, in order to concentrate its "light". And of the white of the eye it is said that it disperses the "light of the eye" and weakens it, so that to look long at a bright white surface, or still more at the sun's light, dazzles "the light of the eye" and effaces it, just as the weak are effaced by the side of the strong. You understand, then, that per-cipient spirit is called light; and why it is so called; and why it is more properly so called. And this is the second signification, that employed by the Few.

You must know, further, that the light of physical sight is [6] marked by several kinds of defects. It sees others but not itself. Again, it does not see what is very distant, nor what is very near, nor what is behind a veil. It sees the exterior of things only, not their interior; the parts, not the whole; things finite, not things infinite. It makes many mistakes in its seeing, for what is large appears to its vision small; what is far, near; what is at rest, motion; what is in motion, at rest. Here are seven defects in-separably attached to the physical eye. If, then, there be such an Eye as is free from all these physical defects, would not *it*, I ask, more properly be given the name of light? Know, then, that there *is* in the mind of man an eye, characterized by just this perfection — that which is variously called Intelligence, Spirit, Human Soul. But we pass over these terms, for the multiplicity of the terms deludes the man of small intelligence into imagining a corresponding multiplicity of ideas. We mean simply that by which the rational man is distinguished from the infant in arms, from the brute beast, and from the lunatic. Let us call it *the Intelligence,* following the current terminology. So, then, the intelligence is more properly called Light than is the eye, just because in capacity it transcends these seven defects.

Take the first. The eye does not behold *itself*, but the intelligence does perceive itself as well as others; and it perceives itself as endowed with knowledge, power, etc., and perceives its own knowledge and perceives its knowledge of its own knowledge, and its knowledge of its knowledge of its own knowledge, and so on *ad infinitum*. Now, this is a property which cannot conceivably be attributed to anything which perceives by means of a physical instrument like the eye. Behind this, however, [7] lies a mystery the unfolding of which would take long.

Take, now, the second defect: the eye does not see what is very near to it nor what is very far away from it; but to the intelligence near and far are indifferent. In the twinkling of an eye it ascends to the highest heaven above, in another instant to the confines of earth beneath. Nay, when the facts are realized, intelligence is revealed as transcending the very idea of "far" and "near", which occur between material bodies; these compass not the precincts of its holiness, for it is a pattern or sample of the attributes of Allāh. Now the sample must be commensurate with the original, even though it does not rise to the degree of equality[1] with it. And this may move you to set your mind to work upon the true meaning of the tradition: "*Allāh created Adam after His own likeness*". But I do not think fit at the present time to go more deeply into the same.

The third defect: the eye does not perceive what is behind the veil, but the intelligence moves freely about the Throne, the Sedile, and everything beyond the veil of the Heavens, and likewise about the Host Supernal, and the Realm Celestial, just as much as about its own world, and its propinquate, (that is its own) kingdom. The realities of things stand unveiled to the intelligence. Its only veil is one which it assumes of its own sake, which resembles the veil that the eye assumes of its own accord in the closing of its eyelids. But we shall explain this more fully in the third chapter of this work.

The fourth defect: the eye perceives only the exterior surfaces of things, but not their interior; nay, the mere moulds and forms, not the realities; while intelligence breaks through into the inwardness of things and into their secrets; apprehends the reality of things and their essential spirit; [8] elicits their causes and laws — from what they had origin, how they were created, of how many ideal forms they are composed, what rank of Being

---

[1] Reading ﺓﺍﻭﺎﺴﻣ, which both sense and rhyme demand.

they occupy, what is their several relation to all other created things, and much else, the exposition of which would take very long; wherein I think good to be brief.

The fifth: the eye sees only a fraction of what exists, for all concepts, and many percepts, are beyond its vision; neither does it apprehend sounds, nor yet smells, nor tastes, nor sensations of hot and cold, nor the percipient faculties, by which I mean the faculties of hearing, of smelling, of tasting; nay, all the inner psychical qualities are unseen to it, joy, pleasure, displeasure, grief, pain, delight, love, lust, power, will, knowledge, and innumerable other existences. Thus it is narrow in its scope, limited in its field of action, unable to pass the confines of the world of colour and form, which are the grossest of all entities; for natural bodies are in themselves the grossest of the categories of being, and colour and form are the grossest of their properties. But the domain of intelligence is the entirety of existence, for it both apprehends the entities we have enumerated, and has free course among all others beside (and they are the major part), passing upon them judgments that are both certain and true. To it, therefore, are the inward secrets of things manifest, and the hidden forms of things clear. Then tell me by what right the physical eye is given equality with the intelligence in claiming the name of Light? No verily! it is only relatively light; but in relation to the intelligence it is darkness. Sight is but one of the spies of Intelligence [9] who sets it to watch the grossest of his treasures, namely, the treasury of colours and forms; bids it carry reports about the same to its Lord, who then judges thereof in accordance with the dictates of his penetration and his judgment. Likewise are all the other faculties but Intelligence's spies — imagination, phantasy, thought, memory, recollection; and behind them are servitors and retainers, constrained to his service in this present world of his. These, I say, he constrains, and among these he moves at will, as freely as monarch constrains his vassals to his service, yea, and more freely still. But to expound this would take us long, and we have already treated of it in the book of my *Ihyā' al-'Ulūm*, entitled "The Marvels of the Mind".

The sixth: the eye does not see what is infinite. What it sees is the attributes of known bodies, and these can only be conceived as finite. But the intelligence apprehends concepts, and concepts cannot be conceived as finite. True, in respect of the knowledge which has actually been attained, the content actually presented to the intelligence is no more than finite, but potentially it does apprehend that which is infinite. It would take too long to explain this fully, but if you desire an example, here is one from arithmetic. In this science the intelligence apprehends the series of integers, which series is infinite; further, it apprehends the coefficients of two, three, and all the other integers, and to these also no limit can be conceived; and it apprehends all the different relations between numbers, and to these also no limit can be conceived; and finally it apprehends its own knowledge of a thing, and its knowledge of its knowledge of its knowledge of that thing; and so on, potentially, to infinity.

The seventh: the eye apprehends the large as small. It sees the sun the size of a bowl, and the stars like silverpieces scattered upon a carpet of azure. But intelligence apprehends that the stars [10] and the sun are larger, times upon times, than the earth. To the eye the stars seem to be standing still, and the boy to be getting no taller. But the intelligence sees the boy moving constantly as he grows; the shadow lengthening constantly; and the stars moving every instant, through distances of many miles. As the Prophet said to Gabriel, asking: "Has the sun moved?" And Gabriel answered: "No — Yes". "How so?" asked he; and the other replied: "Between my saying No and Yes it has moved a distance equal to five hundred years". And so the mistakes of vision are manifold, but the intelligence transcends them all.

Perhaps you will say, we see those who are possessed of intelligence making mistakes nevertheless. I reply, their imaginative and phantastic faculties often pass judgments and form convictions which they think are the judgments of the intelligence. The error is therefore to be attributed to those lower faculties. See my account of all these faculties in my *Mī'ār al-'Ilm* and *Maḥakk al-Naẓar*. But when the intelligence is separated from the deceptions of the phantasy and the imagination, error on its part is inconceivable; it sees things as they are. This separation is, however, difficult, and only attains perfection after death. Then is error unveiled, and then are mysteries brought to light, and each one meets the weal or the woe which he has already laid up for himself, and "*beholds a Book, which reckons each venial and each mortal sin, without omitting a single one*".[1] In that hour it shall be said unto him: "*We have stripped from thee the Veil that covered thee and thy vision this day is iron*".[2] Now that covering Veil is even that of the imagination and the phantasy; and therefore the man who has been deluded by his own fancies, his false beliefs, and his vain imaginations, replies: "*Our Lord! We have seen Thee and heard Thee!* [11] *O send us back and we will do good.*[3] *Verily now we have certain knowledge!*"

From all which you understand that *the eye* may more justly be called Light than the light (so called) which is apprehended by sense; and further that *the intelligence* should more properly be called Light than the eye. It would be even true to say that between these two there exists so great a difference in value, that we may, nay we must, consider only the INTELLIGENCE as deserving the name Light at all.

2. The Koran as the Sun of the Intelligence

Further you must notice here, that while the intelligence of men does truly see, the things it sees are not all upon the same plane. Its knowledge is in some cases, so to speak, *given*, that is, present in the intelligence, as in the case of axiomatic truths, e.g. that the same thing

[1] S. 50, 18.   [2] S. 22, 50.   [3] S. 12, 32.

cannot be both with and without an origin; or existent and non-existent; or that the same proposition cannot be both true and false; or that the judgment which is true of one thing is true of an identically similar thing; or that, granted the existence of the particular, the existence of the universal must necessarily follow.

For example, granted the existence of black, the existence of "colour" follows; and the same with "man" and "animal"; but the converse does not present itself to the intelligence as necessarily true; for "colour" does not involve "black", nor does "animal" involve "man". And there are many other true propositions, some necessary, some contingent, and some impossible. Other propositions, again, do not find the intelligence invariably with them, when they recur to it, but have to shake it up, arouse it, strike flint on steel, in order to elicit its spark. Instances of such propositions are the theorems of speculation, to apprehend which the intelligence has to be aroused by the dialectic (*kalām*) of the philosophers. Thus it is when the light of philosophy dawns that man sees actually, after having before seen potentially. Now the greatest [12] of philosophies is the word (*kalām*) of Allāh in general, and the Koran in particular.

Therefore the verses of the Koran, in relation to intelligence, have the value of sunlight in relation to the eyesight, to wit, it is by this sunlight that the act of seeing is accomplished. And therefore the Koran is most properly of all called Light, just as the light of the sun is called light. The Koran, then, is represented to us by the Sun, and the intelligence by the Light of the Eye, and hereby we understand the meaning of the verse, which saith: "*Believe then on Allāh and His Prophet, and the Light which we caused to descend*"[1]; and again: "*There hath come a sure proof from your Lord, and we have caused a clear Light to descend*".[2]

---

[1] S. 64, 8.
[2] S. 4, 173.

3. The Worlds Visible and Invisible:
with their Lights

You have now realized that there are two kinds of eye, an external and an internal; that the former belongs to one world, the World of Sense, and that internal vision belongs to another world altogether, the World of the Realm Celestial; and that each of these two eyes has a sun and a light whereby its seeing is perfected; and that one of these suns is external, the other internal, the former belonging to the seen world, viz. the sun, which is an object of sense-perception, and the other internal, belonging to the world of the Realm Celestial, viz. the Koran, and other inspired books of Allāh. If, then, this has been disclosed to you thoroughly and entirely, then one of the doors of this Realm Celestial has been opened unto you. In that world there are marvels, in comparison with which this world of sight is utterly contemned. He who never fares to that world, but allows the limitations of life in this lower world of sense to settle upon him, is still a brute beast, an excommunicate from that which constitutes us men; gone astray is he more than any brute beast, for to the brute are not vouched the wings of flight, on which to fly away unto that invisible world. *"Such men"*, the Koran says, *"are cattle, nay, are yet further astray!"*[1] [13] As the rind is to the fruit; as the mould or the form in relation to the spirit; as darkness in relation to light; as infernal to supernal; so is this World of Sense in relation to the world of the Realm Celestial. For this reason the latter is called the World Supernal or the World of Spirit, or the World of Light, in contrast with the World Beneath, the World of Matter and of Darkness. But do not imagine that I mean by the World Supernal the World of the [Seven] Heavens, though they are "above" in respect of part of our world of sense-perception. *These* heavens are equally present to our apprehension, and that of the lower animals. But a man finds the doors of the Realm Celestial closed to him,

[1] S. 7, 178.

neither does he become of or belonging to that Realm unless *"this earth to him be changed into that which is not earth, and likewise the heavens"*[1]; unless, in short, all that comes within the ken of his sense and his imagination, including the visible heavens, cause to be his earth, and his heaven come to be all that transcends his sense. This is the first Ascension for every Pilgrim, who has set out on his Progress to approach the Presence Dominical. Thus mankind was consigned back to the lowest of the low, and must thence rise to the world of highest height. Not so is it with the Angels; for they are part of the World of the Realm Celestial, floating ever in the Presence of the Transcendence, whence they gaze down upon our World Inferior. Thereof spoke the Prophet in the Tradition: *"Allāh created the creation in darkness, then sent an effusion of His light upon it"*, and *"Allāh hath Angels, beings who know the works of men better than they know them themselves"*. Now the Prophets, when their ascents reached unto the World of the Realm Celestial, attained the uttermost goal, and from thence looked down upon a totality of the World Invisible; for he who is in the World of the Realm Celestial is with Allāh, and hath the keys [14] of the Unseen. I mean that from where he is the causes of existing things descend into the World of Sense; for the world of sense is one of the effects of yonder world of cause, resulting from it just as the shadow results from a body, or as fruit from that which fructuates, or as the effect from a cause. Now the key to this knowledge of the effect is sought and found in the cause. And for this reason the World of Sense is a type of the World of the Realm Celestial, as will appear when we explain the NICHE, the LAMP. and the TREE. For the thing compared is in some sort parallel, and bears resemblance, to the thing compared therewith, whether that resemblance be remote or near: a matter, again, which is unfathomably deep, so that whoever has scanned its inner meaning has had revealed to him the verities of the types in the Koran by an easy way.

[1] S. 14, 48.

I said that everything that sees self and not-self deserves more properly the name of Light, while that which adds to these two functions the function of making the not-self visible, still more properly deserves the name of Light than that which has no effect whatever beyond itself. *This* is the light which merits the name of "*Lamp Illuminant*",[1] because its light is effused upon the not-self. Now this is the property of the transcendental prophetic spirit, for through its means are effused the illuminations of the sciences upon the created world. Thus is explained the name given by Allāh to Mohammed, "*Illuminant*".[2] Now all the Prophets are Lamps, and so are the Learned — but the difference between them is incalculable.

4. These Lights as Lamps Terrestrial and Celestial: with their Order and Grades

If it is proper to call that from which the light of vision emanates a "Lamp Illuminant", then that from which the Lamp is itself lit may [15] meetly be symbolized by *Fire*. Now all these Lamps Terrestrial were originally lit from the Light Supernal alone; and of the transcendental Spirit of prophecy it is written that "*Its oil were well-nigh luminous though fire touched it not*"; but becomes "*very light upon light*" when touched by that Fire.[3] Assuredly, then, the kindling source of those Spirits Terrestrial is the divine Spirits Supernal, described by Ali and Ibn Abbas, when they said that "Allāh hath an Angel with countenances seventy thousand, to each countenance seventy thousand mouths, in each mouth seventy thousand tongues wherewith he laudeth God most High". This is he who is contrasted with all the angelic host, in the words: "*On the day whereon* THE SPIRIT *ariseth and the Angels, rank on rank*".[4] These Spirits Celestial, then, if they be considered as the kindling-source of the Lamps

---

[1] S. 33, 46.   [3] S. 24, 35; see p. [45] of translation.
[2] S. 46, 33.   [4] S. 28, 78.

Terrestrial, can be compared alone with "*Fire*".[1] And that kindling is not perceived save "*on the Mountain's side*".[2]

Let us now take these Lights Celestial from which are lit the Lamps Terrestrial, and let us rank them in the order in which they themselves are kindled, the one from the other. Then the nearest to the fountain-head will be of all others the worthiest of the name of Light, for he is the highest in order and rank. Now the analogy for this graded order in the world of sense can only be seized by one who sees the light of the moon coming through the window of a house, falling on a mirror fixed upon a wall, which reflects that light on to another wall, whence it in turn is reflected on the floor, so that the floor becomes illuminated therefrom. The light upon the floor is owed to that upon the wall, and the light on the wall to that in the mirror, and the light in the mirror to that from the moon, and the light in the moon to that from the sun, [16] for it is the sun that radiates its light upon the moon. Thus these four lights are ranged one above the other, each one more perfect than the other; and each one has a certain rank and a proper degree which it never passes beyond. I would have you know, then, that it has been revealed to the men of Insight that even so are the Lights of the Realm Celestial ranged in an order; and that the highest is the one who is nearest to the Ultimate Light. It may well be, then, that the rank of Seraphiel is above the rank of Gabriel; and that among them is that Nighest to Allāh, he whose rank comes nighest to the Presence Dominical which is the Fountain-head of all these lights; and that among these is a Nighest to Man, and that between these two are grades innumerable, whereof all that is known is that they are many, and that they are ordered in rank and grade, and that as they have described themselves, so they are indeed — "*Not one of us but has his determined place and standing*",[3] and "*We are verily the ranked ones; we are they in whose mouth is Praise*".[3]

[1] S. 28, 29.   [2] S. 28, 29; also 19, 53.   [3] S. 37, 164–7.

5. The Source of all these Grades of Light: ALLAH

The next thing I would have you know is that these degrees of light do not ascend in an infinite series, but rise to a final Fountain-head who is Light in and by Himself, upon Whom comes no light from any external source, and from Whom every light is effused according to its order and grade. Ask yourself, now, whether the name Light is more due to that which is illumined and borrows its light from an external source; or to that which in itself is luminous, illuminating all else beside? I do not believe that you can fail to see the true answer, and thus conclude that the name light is most of all due to this LIGHT SUPERNAL, above Whom there is no light at all, and from Whom light descends upon all other things.

Nay, I do not hesitate to say boldly that the term "light" as applied to aught else than this primary light is purely metaphorical; for all [17] others, if considered in themselves, have, in themselves and by themselves, no light at all. Their light is borrowed from a foreign source; which borrowed illumination has not any support in itself, only in something not-itself. But to call the borrower by the same name as the lender is mere metaphor. Think you that the man who borrows riding-habit, saddle, horse, or other riding beast, and mounts the same when and as the lender appoints, is actually, or only metaphorically, rich? The latter, assuredly! The borrower remains in himself as poor as ever, and only of him who made the loan and exacts its return can richness be predicated — him who gave and can take away. Therefore, the Real Light is He in Whose hand lies creation and its destinies; He who first gives the light and afterwards sustains it. He shares with no other the reality of this name, nor the full title to the same; save in so far as He calls some other by that name, deigns to call him by it in the same way as a Liege-Lord deigns to give his vassal a fief, and therewith bestows on him the title of lord. Now when that vassal realizes the truth, he understands that both he and his are the property of his Liege, and of Him alone, a property shared by Him with no partner in the world.

You now know that Light is summed up in *appearing* and *manifesting,* and you have ascertained the various gradations of the same. You must further know that there is no darkness so intense as the darkness of Not-being. For a dark thing is called "dark" simply because it cannot appear to anyone's vision; it never comes to exist for sight, though it does exist in itself. But that which has no existence for others *nor* for itself is assuredly the very extreme of darkness. In contrast with it is Being, which is, therefore, Light; for unless a thing is manifest in itself, [18] it is not manifest to others. Moreover, Being is itself divided into that which has being in itself, and that which derives its being from not-itself. The being of this latter is borrowed, having no existence by itself. Nay, if it is regarded in and by itself, it is pure not-being. Whatever being it has is due to its relation to a not-itself; and this is not real being at all, as you learned from my parable of the Rich and the Borrowed Garment. Therefore, Real Being is Allāh most High, even as Real Light is likewise Allāh.

6. The Mystic Verity of Verities

It is from this starting-point that Allāh's gnostics rise from metaphors to realities, as one climbs from the lowlands to the mountains; and at the end of their Ascent see, as with the direct sight of eye-witnesses, that there is nothing in existence save Allāh alone, and that *"everything perisheth except His Countenance, His Aspect"*[1] (*wajh*); not that it perisheth at some particular moment, but rather it is sempiternally a perishing thing, since it cannot be conceived except as perishing. For each several thing other than Allāh is, when considered in and by itself, pure not-being; and if considered from the "aspect" (*wajh*) to which existence flows from the Prime Reality, it is viewed as existing, but not in itself, solely from the "aspect"

[1] S. 88, 28.

which accompanies Him Who gives it existence. Therefore, the God-aspect is the sole thing in existence. For everything has two aspects, an aspect to itself and an aspect to its Lord: in respect of the first, it is Not-being; but in respect of the God-aspect, it is Being. *Therefore* there is no Existent except God and the God-aspect, and therefore all things are perishing except the God-aspect from and to all eternity. These gnostics, therefore, have no need to await the arising of the Last Uprising in order to hear the Creator proclaim, "*To whom is the power this day? To* ALLAH! *the One, the Not-to-be-withstood*"[1]; [19] for that summons is pealing in their ears always and for ever. Neither do they understand by the cry "Allāh is most great" (*Allāhu akbar*) that He is only "greater" than others. God forbid! For in all existence there is beside Him none for Him to exceed in greatness. No other attains so much as to the degree of co-existence, or of sequent existence, nay of existence at all, except from the Aspect that accompanies Him. All existence is, exclusively, His Aspect. Now it is impossible that He should be "greater" than His own Aspect. The meaning is rather that he is too absolutely Great to be called Greater, or Most Great, by way of relation or comparison — too Great for anyone, whether Prophet or Angel, to grasp the real nature of His Greatness. For none knows Allāh with a real knowledge but He Himself; for every known falls necessarily under the sway and within the province of the Knower; a state which is the very negation of all Majesty, all "Greatness". The full proof whereof I have given in my *al-Maqṣad al-Asnā fī ma'ānī asmā'i-llāhi-l Ḥusnā*.

These gnostics, on their return from their Ascent into the heaven of Reality, confess with one voice that they saw nought existent there save the One Real. Some of them, however, arrived at this scientifically, and others experimentally and subjectively. From these last the plurality of things fell away in its entirety. They were drowned in the absolute Unitude, and their intelligences

---

[1] S. 16, 40.

were lost in Its abyss. Therein became they as dumb-foundered things. No capacity remained within them save to recall ALLAH; yea, not so much as the capacity to recall their own selves. So there remained nothing with them save ALLAH. They became drunken with a drunkenness wherein the sway of their own intelligence disappeared; so that one[1] exclaimed, "I am The ONE REAL!" and another, "Glory be to ME! How great is MY glory!"[2] and another, "Within this robe is nought but Allāh!"... But the words of Lovers Passionate in their intoxication and ecstacy [20] must be hidden away and not spoken of... Then when that drunkenness abated and they came again under the sway of the intelligence, which is Allāh's balance-scale upon earth, they knew that that had not been actual Identity, but only something resembling Identity; as in those words of the Lover at the height of his passion:

"I am He whom I love and He whom I love is I;
We are two spirits immanent in one body".[3]

For it is possible for a man who has never seen a mirror in his life, to be confronted suddenly by a mirror, to look into it, and to think that the form which he sees in the mirror *is* the form of the mirror itself, "identical" with it. Another might see wine in a glass, and think that the wine is just the stain of the glass. And if that thought becomes with him use and wont, like a fixed idea with him, it absorbs him wholly, so that he sings:

"The glass is thin, the wine is clear!
The twain are alike the matter is perplexed:
For 'tis as though there were wine and no wine-glass
there,
Or as though there were wine-glass and nought of wine!"

Here there is a difference between saying, "The wine *is* the wine-glass", and saying, " 'tis *as though it were* the wine-glass". Now, when this state prevails, it is called in relation to him who experiences it, Extinction, nay, Ex-

---

[1] Al-Ḥallāj.

[2] Abū Yazīd al-Bisṭāmī. See Massignon's *Ḥallāj*, p. 513.

[3] By al-Ḥallāj.

tinction of Extinction, for the soul has become extinct to itself, extinct to its own extinction; for it becomes unconscious of itself and unconscious of its own unconsciousness, since, were it conscious of its own unconsciousness, it would be conscious of itself. In relation to the man immersed in this state, the state is called, in the language of metaphor, "Identity"; in the language of reality, "Unification". And beneath these verities also lie mysteries which we are not at liberty to discuss.

7. The "God-Aspect": an "advanced" explanation of the relation of these Lights to ALLAH

It may be that you desire greatly to know the aspect (*wajh*) [21] whereby Allāh's light is related to the heavens and the earth, or rather the aspect whereby He is in Himself the Light of heavens and earth. And this shall assuredly not be denied you, now that you know that Allāh is Light, and that beside Him there is no light, and that He is every light, and that He is the universal light: since light is an expression for that by which things are revealed or, higher still, that by and for which they are revealed; yea, and higher still, that by, for, and from which they are revealed: and now that you know, too that, of everything called light, only that by, for, and from which things are revealed is *real* — that Light beyond which there is no light to kindle and feed its flame, for It is kindled and fed in Itself, from Itself, and for Itself, and from no other source at all. Such a conception, such a description, you are now assured, can be applied to the Great Primary alone. You are also assured that the heavens and the earth are filled with light appertaining to those two fundamental light-planes, our *Sight* and our *Insight*; by which I mean our *senses* and our *intelligence*. The first kind of light is what we see in the heavens — sun and moon and stars; and what we see in earth — that is, the rays which are poured over the whole face of the earth, making visible all the different colours and hues, especially in the season of spring; and over all animals and plants and things, in all their states: for without these rays no colour would appear or even exist. Moreover, every shape and size which is visible to perception is apprehended in consequence of colour, and it is impossible to conceive of apprehending them without colour. As for the other ideal, intelligential Lights, the World Supernal is filled with them — to wit, the angelic substances; and the World Inferior is also full of them — [22] to wit, animal life and human life successively. The order of the World Inferior is manifested by means of this inferior human light; while the order of the World Supernal is manifested by means of that angelical light. This is the order alluded to in the passage in the Koran, "*He it is Who has formed you from the earth, and hath peopled it with you, that He might call you Successors upon the earth*" . . . and "*Maketh you Successors on the earth*", and "*Verily I have set in the earth a Successor*" (*Khalīfa*).[1]

Thus you see that the whole world is all filled with the external lights of perception, and the internal lights of intelligence; also that the lower lights are effused or emanate the one from the other, as light emanates or is effused from a lamp; while the Lamp itself is the transcendental Light of Prophecy; and that the transcendental Spirits of Prophecy are lit from the Spirit Supernal, as the lamp is lit from fire; and that the Supernals are lit the one from the other; and that their order is one of ascending grades: further, that these all rise to the Light of Lights, the Origin and Fountainhead of lights, and that is ALLAH, only and alone; and that all other lights are borrowed from Him, and that His alone is real light; and that everything is from His light, nay, He is everything, nay, HE IS THAT HE IS, none but He has ipseity or heity at all, save by metaphor. Therefore there is no light but He, while all other lights are only lights from the Aspect which accompanies Him, not from themselves. Thus the aspect and face of everything faces to Him and turns in His direction; and "*whithersoever they*

---

[1] S. 61, 11; 55, 24; 62, 27; 30, 2. Cf. *Mishkāt*, p. [34].

turn themselves there is the Face of Allāh".[1] So, then, there is no divinity but HE; for "*di*vinity" is an expression by which is connoted that towards which all faces are *di*rected"[2] in worship and in confession that He is Deity; but which I mean the faces of the *hearts* of men, for they verily are lights and spirits. Nay, more, just as "there is no *deity* but He", so there is no *heity* but He, [23] for "he" is an expression for something which one can indicate; but in every and any case we can but indicate HIM. Every time you indicate anything, your indication is, in reality, to Him, even though through your ignorance of the truth of truths which we have mentioned you know it not. Just as one cannot point to, indicate, *sunlight* but only the *sun*, so the relation of the sum of things to Allāh is, in the visible analogue, as the relation of light to the sun. Therefore "*There is no deity but* ALLAH" is the Many's declaration of Unity: that of the Few is "*There is no he but* HE"; the former is more general, but the latter is more particular, more comprehensive, more exact, and more apt to give him who declares it entrance into the pure and absolute Oneness and Onliness. This kingdom of the One-and-Onliness is the ultimate point of mortals' Ascent: there is no ascending stage beyond it; for "ascending" involves plurality, being a sort of relatively involving two stages, an ascent *from* and an ascent *to*. But when Plurality has been eliminated, Unity is established, relation is effaced, all indication from "here" to "there" falls away, and there remains neither height nor depth, nor anyone to fare up or down. The upward Progress, the Ascent of the soul, then becomes impossible, for there is no height beyond the Highest, no plurality alongside of the One, and, now that plurality has terminated, no Ascent for the soul. If there be, indeed, any change, it is by way of the "Descent into the Lowest Heaven", the radiation from above downwards; for the Highest,

[1] S. 2, 115, see 144, 149, 150.

[2] Gh.'s piece of amateur etymology here, by which he appears to derive the root *'lh* ("god") from the root *wly* ("turn"), is about as absurd as my attempt to suggest it in the English.

125

though It may have no higher, has a lower. This is the goal of goals, the last object of spiritual search, known of him who knows it, denied by him who is ignorant of it. It belongs to that knowledge which is according to the form of the hidden thing, and which no one knoweth save the Learned[1] is Allāh, If, therefore, they utter it, it is only denied by the Ignorant of Him.

There is no improbability in the explanation given by these Learned to this "Descent into the Lowest Heaven", [24] namely, that it is the descent of *an Angel*; though one of those Gnostics[2] has, indeed, fancied a less probable explanation. He, immersed as he was in the divine One-and-Onliness, said that *Allāh* has "a descent into the lowest heaven", and that this descent is *His* descent, in order to use physical senses, and to set in motion bodily limbs; and that *He* is the one indicated in the Tradition in which the Prophet says, "*I have become His hearing whereby He heareth, His vision whereby He seeth, His tongue wherewith He speaketh*".[3] Now if the Prophet was Allāh's hearing and vision and tongue, then *Allāh* and He alone is the Hearer, the Seer, the Speaker; and *He* is the one indicated in His own word to Moses, "*I was sick, and thou visitedst Me not*".[4] According to this, the bodily movements of this Confessor of the divine Unity are from the lowest heaven; his sensations from a heaven next above; and his intelligence from the heaven next above that. From that heaven of the intelligence he fares upward to the limit of the Ascension of created things, the kingdom of the One-and-Onliness, a sevenfold way; thereafter "*settleth he himself on the throne*" of the divine Unity, and therefrom "*taketh command*"[5] throughout his storied heavens. Well might one, in looking upon such an one, apply to him the saying, "*Allāh created Adam after the image*

[1] Cf. S. 3, 7.
[2] Al-Ḥallāj.
[3] A saying reported by Ibn Adham, d. 170.
[4] See St. Matt. xxv.
[5] Ar. *al amr*. See on p. [55], Introduction, pp. 94–102. Or, "controlleth things". And see S. 32, 5.

of the Merciful One"; until, after contemplating that word more deeply, he becomes aware that it has an interpretation like those other words, "I am the ONE REAL", "Glory be to ME!"[1] or those sayings of the Prophet, that Allāh said, "*I was sick and thou visitedst Me not*", and "*I am His hearing, and His vision, and His tongue*". But I see fit now to draw rein in this exposition, for I think that you cannot bear more of this sort than the amount which I have now communicated.

8. The Relation of these Lights to ALLAH: Simpler Illustrations and Explanations

It may well be that you will not rise to the height of these words, for all your pains; it may be that for all your pains you will come short of it after all. Here, then, is something that lies nearer your understanding, and nearer your weakness. The meaning of the doctrine that Allāh is [25] the Light of Heavens and Earth may be understood in relation to phenomenal, visible light. When you see hues of spring — the tender green, for example — in the full light of day, you entertain no doubt but that you are looking on colours, and very likely you suppose that you are looking on nothing else alongside of them. As though you should say, "I see nothing alongside of the green". Many have, in fact, obstinately maintained this. They have asserted that light is a meaningless term, and that there *is* nothing but colour with the colours. Thus they denied the existence of the light, although it was the most manifest of all things — how should it not be so, considering that through it alone all things become manifest?, for it is the thing that is itself visible and makes visible, as we said before. But, when the sun sank, and heaven's lamp disappeared from sight, and night's shadow fell, then apprehended these men the existence of an essential difference between inherent shadow and inherent light; and they confessed that light is a form that lies behind all colour, and is apprehended with colour,

[1] M., p. [19].

127

insomuch that, so to speak, through its intense union with the colours it is not apprehended, and through its intense obviousness it is invisible. And it may be that this very intensity is the direct cause of its invisibility, for things that go beyond one extreme pass over to the extreme opposite.

If this is clear to you, you must further know that those endowed with this Insight never saw a single object without seeing Allāh along with it. It may be that one of them went further than this and said, "I have never seen a single object, but I first saw Allāh"; for some of them only see objects through and in Allāh, while others first see objects and then see Allāh in and through those objects. It is to the first class that the Koran alludes to in the words, "*Doth it not suffice that thy Lord seeth all?*"[1] and to the second in the words, "*We shall shew them our signs in all the world and in themselves*".[1] For the first class [26] have the direction intuition of Allāh, and the second infer Him from His works. The former is the rank of the Saint-Friends of God, the latter of the Learned "*who are stablished in knowledge*".[2] After these two grades there remains nothing except that of the careless, on whose faces is the veil.

Thus you see that just as everything is manifest to man's Sight by means of light, so everything is manifest to man's Insight by means of Allāh; for He is *with* everything every moment and by Him does everything appear. But here the analogy ceases, and we have a radical difference; namely, that phenomenal light can be conceived of as disappearing with the sinking of the sun, and as assuming a veil in order that shadow may appear: while the divine light, which is the condition of all appearance, cannot be conceived as disappearing. That sun can never set! It abides for ever with all things. Thus the method of difference (as a method for the demonstration of the Existence of God from His works) is not at our disposal. Were the appearance of Allāh conceivable,

[1] S. 41, 53.
[2] S. 3, 6.

heaven and earth would fall to ruin, and thence, through difference, would be apprehended an effect which would simultaneously compel the recognition of the Cause whereby all things appeared. But, as it is, all Nature remains the same and invariable to our sight because of the unity of its Creator, for "*all things are singing His praise*"[1] (not some things) at *all* times (not sometimes); and thus the method of difference is eliminated, and the way to the knowledge of God is obscured. For the most manifest way to the knowledge of things is by their contraries: the thing that possesses no contrary and no opposite, its features being always exactly alike when you are looking at it, will very likely elude your notice altogether. In this case its obscureness results from its very obviousness, and its elusiveness from the very radiance of its brightness. Then glory to Him who hides Himself from His own creation by His utter manifestness, and is veiled from their gaze through the very effulgence of His own light!

But it may be that not even this teaching is intelligible to some limited intelligences, [27] who from our statement (that "Allāh is *with* everything", as the light is with everything) will understand that He is in every *place*. Too high and holy is He to be related to place! So far from starting this vain imagining, we assert to you that He is prior to everything, and above everything, and that He makes everything manifest. Now manifester is inseparable from manifested, subjectively, in the cognition of the thinker; and this is what we mean by saying that Allāh accompanies or is "with" everything. You know, further, that manifester is prior to, and above, manifested, though He be "with" it; but he is "with" it from one aspect, and "above" it from another. You are not to suppose, therefore, that there is here any contradiction. Or, consider, how in the world of sense, which is the highest to which your knowledge can rise, the motion of your hands goes "with" the motion of its

[1] See S. 17, 44.

129

shadow, and yet is prior to it as well. And whoever has not wit enough to see this, ought to abandon these researches altogether; for

> "To every science its own people;
> And each man finds easy that for which he has been
> created apt".

PART II. — THE SCIENCE OF SYMBOLISM

PROLEGOMENA TO THE EXPLANATION OF THE SYMBOLISM OF THE NICHE, THE LAMP, THE GLASS, THE TREE, THE OIL, AND THE FIRE

The exposition of this symbolism involves, first of all, two cardinal considerations, which afford limitless scope for investigation, but to which I shall merely allude very briefly here.

First, the science and method of symbolism; the way in which the spirit of the ideal form[1] is captured by the mould of the symbol; the mutual relationship of the two; the inner nature of this correspondence between the world of Sense (which supplies the clay of the moulds, the material of the symbolism) and the world of the Realm Supernal from which the Ideas descend.[2]

Second, the gradations of the several spirits of our mortal clay, and the degree [28] of light possessed by each. For we treat of this latter symbolism in order to explain the former.

(i) THE OUTWARD AND THE INWARD IN SYMBOLISM: TYPE AND ANTITYPE

The world is Two Worlds, spiritual and material, or, if you will, a World Sensual and a World Intelligential; or again, if you will, a World Supernal and a World Inferior. All these expressions are near each other, and

[1] Or Idea = in practically the Platonic sense.

[2] (By Ghazzālī). In this Light-Verse, in Ibn Mas'ūd's reading, the words "in the heart of the believer" follow the words "of His light". And Ubayy b. Ka'b's, instead of "the similitude of His light", has "the similitude of the light of the heart of him who believes is like", etc.

the difference between them is merely one of viewpoint. If you regard the two worlds in themselves, you use the first expression; if in respect of the organ which apprehends them, the second; if in respect of their mutual relationship, the third. You may, perhaps, also term them the World of Dominance and Sense-perception, and, the World of the Unseen and the Realm Supernal. It were no marvel if the students of the realities underlying the terminology were puzzled by the multiplicity of these terms, and imagined a corresponding multiplicity of ideas. But he to whom the realities beneath the terms are disclosed makes the ideas primary and the terms secondary: while inferior minds take the opposite course. To them the term is the source from which the reality proceeds. We have an allusion to these two types of mind in the Koran, "*Whether is the more rightly guided, he who walks with his face bent down, or he who walks in a straight Way, erect?*"[1]

1. The two Worlds: their types and antitypes

Such is the idea of the Two Worlds. And the next thing for you to know is, that the supernal world of "the Realm" is a world invisible to the majority of men; and the world of our senses is the world of perception, because it is perceived of all. This World Sensual is the point from which we ascend to [29] the world Intelligential; and, but for this connexion between the two, and their reciprocal relationship, the way upward to the higher sphere would be barred. And were this upward way impossible, then would the Progress to the Presence Dominical and the near approach to Allāh be impossible too. For no man shall approach near unto Allāh, unless his foot stand at the very centre of the Fold of the Divine Holiness. Now by this World of the "Divine *Holiness*" we mean the world that *transcends* the apprehension of the senses and the imagination. And it is in respect of the law of that world — the law that the soul which is a stranger to it neither goeth out therefrom, nor entereth therein —

[1] S. 67, 22.

that we call it the Fold of the Divine Holiness and Transcendence. And the human spirit, which is the channel of the manifestations of the Transcendence, may be perhaps called "*the Holy Valley*".[1]

Again, this Fold comprises lesser folds, some of which penetrate more deeply than others into the ideas of the Divine Holiness. But the term Fold embraces all the gradations of the lesser ones; for you must not suppose that these terms are enigmas, unintelligible to men of Insight. But I cannot pursue the subject further, for I see that my preoccupation with citing and explaining all this terminology is turning me from my theme. It is for you to apply yourself now to the study of the terms.

To return to the subject we were discussing: the visible world is, as we said, the point of departure up to the world of the Realm Supernal; and the "Pilgrim's Progress of the Straight Way"[2] is an expression for that upward course, which may also be expressed by The Faith", "the Mansions of Right Guidance". Were there no relation between the two worlds, no inter-connexion at all, then all upward progress would be inconceivable from one to the other. Therefore, the divine mercy gave to the World Visible a correspondence with the World of the Realm Supernal, and for this reason there is not a single thing in this world of sense that is not a symbol of something in yonder one. It may well happen that some one thing in this world may symbolize several things in the World of the Realm Supernal, and equally well that some one thing in the latter may have several symbols [30] in the World Visible. We call a thing typical or symbolic when it resembles and corresponds to its antitype under some aspect.

A complete enumeration of these symbols would involve our exhausting the whole of the existing things in both of the Two Worlds! Such a task our mortal power can never fulfil; our human faculties have not sufficed to comprehend it in the past; and with our little lives we

[1] S. 20, 12.   [2] See S. 1, 4.

cannot expound it fully in the present. The utmost I can do is to explain to you a single example. The greater may then be inferred from the less; for the door of research into the mysteries of this knowledge will then lie open to you.

2. An Example of Symbolism, from the Story of Abraham in the Koran

Listen now. If the World of the Realm Supernal contains Light-substances, high and lofty, called "Angels", from which substances the various lights are effused upon the various mortal spirits, and by reason of which these angels are called "lords", then is Allāh "Lord of lords", and these lords will have differing grades of luminousness. The symbols, then, of these in the visible world will be, pre-eminently, the Sun, the Moon, and the Stars. And the Pilgrim of the Way rises first of all to a degree corresponding to that of a *star*. The effulgence of that star's light appears to him. It is disclosed to him that the entire world beneath adores its influence and the effulgence of its light. And so, because of the very beauty and superbness of the thing, he is made aware of something which cries aloud saying, "*This is my Lord!*"[1] He passes on; and as he becomes conscious of the light-degree next above it, namely, that symbolized by *the moon*, lo! in the aerial canopy he beholds that star set, to wit, in comparison with its superior; and he saith, "*Nought that setteth do I adore!*" And so he rises till he arrives at last at the degree symbolized by *the sun*. This, again, he sees is greater and higher than the former, but nevertheless admits of comparison therewith, in virtue of a relationship between the two: [31] But to bear relationship to what is imperfect carries with it imperfection — the "setting" of our allegory. And by reason thereof he saith: "*I have turned my face unto That Who made the heavens and the earth! I am a true believer, and not of those who associate other gods with Allāh!*" Now what is meant to be conveyed by this "THAT WHO" is the vaguest kind of

[1] See for this whole passage S. 6, 75–8.

indication, destitute of all relation or comparison. For, were anyone to ask, "What is the symbol comparable with or corresponding to this That?" no answer to the question could be conceived. Now He Who transcends all relations is ALLAH, the ONE REALITY. Thus, when certain Arabs once asked the Apostle of God, "To what may we relate Allāh?" this reply was revealed, "*Say, He, Allāh is one! His days are neither ended nor begun; neither is He a father nor a son; and none is like unto Him, no not one*"[1]; the meaning of which verse is simply that He transcends relation. Again, when Pharaoh said to Moses: "*What, pray, is the Lord of the Universe?*" as though demanding to know His essence, Moses, in his reply, merely indicated *His works*, because these were clearer to the mind of his interrogator; and answered, "*The Lord of the heavens and the earth*".[2] But Pharaoh said to his courtiers, "*Ha! marked ye that!*" as though objecting to Moses' evasion of his demand to be told Allāh's essential nature. Then Moses said, "*Your Lord, and your first fathers' Lord*". Pharaoh then set him down as insane. He had demanded an analogue, for the description of the divine Essence, and Moses replied to him from His works. And so Pharaoh said, "*Your prophet who has been sent you is insane*".

3. Fundamental Examples of Symbolism: especially from the Story of Moses in the Koran

Let us now return to the pattern we selected for illustrating the symbolic method. The science of the Interpretation of Visions determines for us the value of each kind of symbol; for "Vision is a part of Prophecy". It is clear, is it not, that the *sun*, when seen in a vision, must be interpreted by a Sovereign Monarch, because of their mutual resemblance and their share in a common spiritual idea, to wit, sovereignty over all, and the emanation or effusion of influence and light on to all. The

[1] S. 112.

[2] For this passage see S. 26, 24–7, and for the whole thought compare pp. [54, 55].

antitype of the *moon* will be that Sovereign's Minister; for it is through the moon that the sun sheds his light on the world in its own absence; and even so, it is through his own Minister that the Sovereign [32] makes his influence felt by subjects who never beheld the royal person. Again, the dreamer who sees himself with a ring on his finger with which he seals the mouths of men and the secrets of women, is told that the sign means the early Call to Prayer in the month of Ramadan.[1] Again, for one who sees himself pouring olive oil into an olive-tree the interpretation is that the slave-girl he has wedded is his mother, unrecognized by him. But it is impossible to exhaust the different ways by which symbols of this description may be interpreted, and I cannot set myself the task of enumerating them. I can merely say that just as certain beings of the Spirit-World Supernal are symbolized by Sun, Moon, and Stars, others may be typified by different symbols, when the point of connexion is some characteristic other than light.

For example, if among those beings of that Spirit-World there be something that is fixed and unchangeable; great and never diminishing; from which the waters of knowledge, the excellencies of revelations, issue into the heart, even as waters well out into a valley; It would be symbolized by the *Mountain*.[1] Further, if the beings that are the recipients of those excellencies are of diverse grades, they would be symbolized by the *Valley*; and if those excellencies, on reaching the hearts of men, pass from heart to heart, these hearts are also symbolized by *Valleys*.[2] The head of the Valley will represent the hearts of Prophet, Saint, and Doctor, followed by those who come after them. So, then, if these valleys are lower than the first one, and are watered from it, then that first one will certainly be the "*Right*" *Valley*,[3] because of its

---

[1] Because after the *idhān*, just before morning, food and sexual intercourse are fasted from till the next sunset.

[1] S. 28, 29, 46.   [2] S. 13, 18.   [3] S. 28, 30. See S. 19, 53, and 20, 82.

signal rightness[1] and superiority. And finally will come the lowest valley which receives its water from the last and lowest level of that "Right" Valley, and is accordingly watered from "*the margin of the Right Valley*",[2] not [33] from its deepest part and centre.

But if the spirit of a prophet is typified by a lighted *Lamp*, lit by means of Inspiration ("*We have inspired thee with [a] Spirit from Our power*"),[3] then the symbol of the source of that kindling is *Fire*. If some of those who derive knowledge from the prophets live by a merely traditional acceptance of what they are told, and others by a gift of insight, then the symbol for the former, who investigate nothing, is a *Fire-brand* or a *Torch* or a *Meteor*; while the man of spiritual experience, who has therefore something in some sort common with the prophets, is accordingly symbolized by the *Warming of Fire*, for a man is not warmed by hearing about fire but by being close to it.

If the first stage of prophets is their translation into the World of Holy Transcendence away from the disturbances of senses and imagination, that stage is symbolized by "*the Holy Valley*".[4] And if that Holy Valley may not be trodden save after the doffing of the Two Worlds (that is, this world and the world beyond) and the soul's turning of her face towards the One Real (for this world and the world beyond are co-relatives and both are accidentia of the human light-substance, and can be doffed at one time and donned at another), then the symbol of the putting-off of these Two Worlds is the *doffing of his two sandals* by the pilgrim to Mekka,[5] what time he changes his worldly garments for the pilgrim's robe and faces towards the holy Kaaba.

Nay, but let us now translate ourselves to the Presence Dominical once more, and speak of its symbols. If that Presence hath something whereby the several divine

---

[1] Ghazzālī here plays on the word *ayman*, the root of which means *dexter* or *felix*.
[2] S. 28, 30.   [3] S. 42, 52.   [4] S. 20, 12, and 79, 16.   [5] S. 20, 12.

sciences are engraven on the tablets of hearts susceptible to them, that something will be symbolized by the *Pen*.[1] That within those hearts whereon these things are engraved will be typified by the *Tablet*,[2] *Book*,[3] and *Scroll*.[4] [34] If there be, above the pen that writes, something which constrains it to service, its type will be the *Hand*.[5] If the Presence which embraces Hand and Tablet, Pen and Book, is constituted according to a definite order, It will be typified by the *Form* or *Image*.[6] And if the human form has *its* definite order, after that likeness, then is it created "*in the Image, the Form, of the Merciful One*". Now there is a difference between saying, "In the image of the *Merciful One*", and, "In the image of *Allāh*". For it was the Divine *Mercy* that caused the image of the Divine Presence to be in that "Image". And then Allāh, out of his grace and *mercy*, gave to Adam a summary "image" or "form", embracing every genus and species in the whole world, inasmuch that it was as if Adam were all that was in the world, or were the summarized copy of the world. And Adam's form — this summarized "image" — was inscribed in the handwriting of Allāh, so that *Adam* is the Divine handwriting, which is not the characters of letters (for His Handwriting transcends both characters and letters, even as his Word transcends sound and syllables, and His Pen transcends Reed and Steel, and His Hand transcends flesh and bone). Now, but for this *mercy*, every son of Adam would have been powerless to know his Sovereign-Lord; for "only he who knows himself knows his Lord". This, then, being an effect of the divine mercy, it was "in the image *of the Merciful One*", not "in the image of Allāh", that Adam was created. So, then, the Presence of the Godhead is not the same as the Presence of The Merciful One, nor as the Presence of The Kingship, nor as the Presence of the Sovereign-Lordship; for which reason He commanded us to invoke the protec-

---

[1] S. 68.   [2] S. 85, 22 and 7, 44.   [3] S. 2, 1.   [4] S. 25, 3.
[5] S. 48, 36.   [6] S. 82, 8; cf. 64, 3.

tion of all these Presences severally. *"Say, I invoke the protection of the Lord of mankind, the King of mankind, the Deity of mankind!"*[1] If this idea did not underlie the expression [35] "Allāh created man in the image of the Merciful", the words would be linguistically incorrect; they should then have run, "after His image".[2] But the words, according to Bokhari, run, "After the image of the Merciful".

But as the distinction between the Presence of the Kingship and the Presence of the Lordship call for a long exposition, we must pass on, and be content with the foregoing specimen of the symbolic method. For indeed it is a shoreless sea.

But if you are conscious of a certain repulsion from this symbolism, you may comfort yourself by the text, *"He sent down from heaven rain, and it flowed in the valleys, according to their capacity"*[3]; for the commentaries on this text tell us that the Water here is *knowledge*, and the Valleys are *the hearts of men*.

4. The Permanent Validity of the Outward and Visible Sign: an Example

Pray do not assume from this specimen of symbolism and its method that you have any licence from me to ignore the outward and visible form, or to believe that it has been annulled; as though, for example, I had asserted that Moses had not really shoes on, or did not really hear himself addressed by the words, *"Put thy shoes from off thy feet"*.[4] God forbid! The annulment of the outward and visible sign is the tenet of the Spiritualists (*Bāṭiniyya*), who looked, utterly one-sidedly, at one world, the Unseen, and were grossly ignorant of the balance that exists between it and the Seen. This aspect they wholly failed to understand. Similarly annulment of the inward and invisible meaning is the opinion of the

[1] S. 114.   [2] And *so* they are quoted on p. [7].   [3] S. 13, 19.
[4] S. 20, 12.

Materialists (*Hashawiyya*). In other words, whoever abstracts and isolates the outward from the whole is a Materialist, and whoever abstracts the inward is a Spiritualist, while he who joins the two together is catholic, perfect. For this reason the Prophet said, "The Koran has an outward and an inward, an ending and a beginning" (a Tradition which is, however, possibly traceable to 'Alī, as its pedigree stops short at his name). I assert, on the contrary, that Moses understood from the command "*Put off thy shoes*" the Doffing of the Two Worlds, and obeyed the command *literally* by putting off his two sandals, and *spiritually* by putting off the Two Worlds. Here you just have this cross-relation between the two, [36] the crossing over from one to the other, from outward word to inward idea. The difference between the true and false positions may be thus illustrated. One man hears the word of the Prophet, "The angels of Allāh enter not a house wherein is a dog or a picture", and yet keeps a dog in the house, because, he says, "The outward sense is not what was meant; but the Prophet only meant, 'Turn the dog of Wrath out of the house of the Heart, because Wrath hinders the knowledge which comes from the Lights Angelical; for anger is the demon of the heart'." While the other *first* carries out the command literally, and *then* says, "Dog is not dog because of his visible form, but because of the inner idea of dog — ferocity, ravenousness. If my house, which is the abode of my person, of my body, must be kept clear of doggishness in concrete form, how much more must the house of my heart, which is the abode of man's true and proper essence, be kept clear of doggishness in spiritual idea!" The man, in fact, who combines the two things, he is the perfect man; which is what is meant when it is said, "The perfect man is the one who does not let the light of his knowledge quench the light of his reverence". In the same way he is never seen permitting himself to ignore one single ordinance of religion, for all the perfection of his spiritual Insight. Such a thing is grievous error; and example of which is the evil which befel some mystics, who called it lawful to put-by literal prescriptions of the Shariat as you roll up and put-by a carpet; insomuch that one of them perhaps went so far as to give up the ordinance of prayer, saying, forsooth, that he was always at prayer in his heart! But this is different from the error of those fools of Antinomians (*Ibāḥiyya*) who trifle with sophisms, like the saying of one, "Allāh has no need of our works"; or of another, "The heart is full of vices from which it cannot possibly be cleansed", [37] and did not even desire to eradicate anger and lust, because he believes he is [not] (?) commanded to eradicate them. These last verily, are the follies of fools; but, as for the first-named error, it reminds one of the stumble of a high-bred horse, the error of a mystic whom the devil has diverted from the way and "*drawn him with delusion as with cords*".[1]

To return to our discussion of "the Putting-off of the Shoes". The outward word wakens one to the inward signification, the Putting-off of the Two Worlds. The outward symbol is a real thing, and its application to the inward meaning is a real truth. Every real thing has its corresponding real truth. Those who have realized this are the souls who have attained the degree of the Transparent Glass (we shall see the meaning of this presently). For the Imagination, which supplies, so to speak, the clay from which the symbol is formed, is hard and gross; it conceals the secret meanings; it is interposed between you and the unseen lights. But once let it be clarified, and it becomes like transparent glass, and no longer keeps out the light, but on the contrary becomes a light-conductor, nay, that which keeps that light from being put out by gusts of wind. The story of the Transparent Glass, however, is coming; meanwhile, remember that the gross lower world of the imagination became to the Prophets of God like a transparent "glass" shade and "a niche for lights"; a strainer, filtering clear the divine secrets; a stepping-stone to the World Supernal.

[1] S. 7, 21.

Whereby we may know that the visible symbol is real: and behind it lies a mystery. The same holds good with the symbols of "the Mountain", "the Fire", and the rest.

5. Another Example of this Two-sided and Equal Validity of Outward and Inward

When the Prophet said, "I saw Abdul-Raḥmān enter Paradise crawling", you are not to suppose that he did not see him thus with his own eyes. No, awake he saw him, as a sleeper might see him in a dream, even though the person of Abdul-Raḥmān b. 'Awf was at the time asleep in his house. [38] The only effect of sleep in this and similar visions is to suppress the authority of the senses over the soul, which is the inward light divine; for the senses preoccupy the soul, drag it back to the Sense-world, and turn a man's face away from the world of the Invisible and of the Realm Supernal. But, with the suppression of sense, some of the lights prophetical may become clarified and prevail, inasmuch as the senses are no longer dragging the soul back to their own world, nor occupy their whole attention. And so it sees in waking what others see in sleep. But if it has attained absolute perfection, it is not limited to apprehending the visible form merely; it passes direct from that to the inner idea, and it is disclosed to such an one that faith is drawing the soul of an Abdul-Raḥmān to the World Above (described by the word "Paradise"), while wealth and riches are drawing it down to this present life, the World Below. If the influences which draw it to the preoccupations of this world are more stubborn than those which draw it to the other world, the soul is wholly turned away from its journey to Paradise. But if the attraction of faith is stronger, the soul is merely occasioned difficulty, or retarded, in its course, and the symbol for this in the world of sense is *a crawl*. It is thus that mysteries are shown forth from behind the crystal transparencies of the imagination. Nor is this limited to the Prophet's judgment about Abdul-Raḥmān only, though it was only him he saw at that time. He passes judgment therein on every man whose spiritual vision is strong, whose faith is firm, but whose wealth has so much multiplied that it threatens to crowd out his faith, only failing to do so because the power of that faith more than counter-balances it. This example illustrates to you the way in which prophets used to see concrete objects, and have immediate vision of the spiritual ideas behind them. Most frequently the idea is presented to their direct inward vision *first*, and then looks down from thence on to [39] the imaginative spirit and receives the imprint of some concrete object, analogous to the idea. What is con-ferred by inspiration in sleeping vision or dreams needs interpretation.[1]

(ii) THE PSYCHOLOGY OF THE HUMAN SOUL: ITS FIVE FACULTIES OR SPIRITS

The gradations of human Spirits Luminous; in knowing which we may know the symbolism of the Light-Verse in the Koran.

The *first* of these is the *sensory spirit*. This is the recipient of the information brought in by the senses; for it is the root and origin of the animal spirit, and constitutes the differentia of the animal genus. It is found in the infant at the breast.

The *second* is the *imaginative spirit*. This is the recorder of the information conveyed by the senses. It keeps that in-formation filed and ready to hand, so as to present it to the intelligential spirit above it, when the information is called for. It is not found in the infant at the beginning of its evolution. This is why an infant wants to get hold of a thing when he sees it, while he forgets about it when it is out of his sight. No conflict of desire arises in his soul for something out of sight until he gets a little older, when he begins to cry for it and asks to have it, because its image

[1] (*Note by Ghazzālī*). The proportion borne by dreams to the other characteristics of prophethood is as one to forty-six. That borne by waking vision has a greater ratio — as one to three, I believe, for it has been revealed to us that the prophetic characteristics fall defi-nitely into three categories, and of these three one is waking vision.

is still with him, preserved in his imagination. This faculty is possessed by some, but not all animals. It is not found, for example, in the moth which perishes in the flame. [40] The moth makes for the flame, because of its desire for the sunlight, and, thinking that the flame is a window opening to the sunlight, it hurries on to the flame, and injures itself. Yet, if it flies on into the dark, back it comes again, time after time. Now had it the mnemonic spirit, which gives permanence to the sensation of pain that is conveyed by the tactile sense, it would not return to the flame after being hurt once by it. On the other hand, the dog that has received one whipping runs away whenever it sees the stick again.

Third, the *intelligential spirit*. This apprehends ideas beyond the spheres of sense and imagination. It is the specifically human faculty. It is not found in the lower animals, nor yet in children. The objects of its apprehension are axioms of necessary and universal application, as we mentioned in the section in which the light of intelligence was given precedence over that of the eye.

Fourth, the *discursive spirit*. This takes the data of pure reason and combines them, arranges them as premises, and deduces from them informing knowledge. Then it takes, for example, two conclusions thus learned, combines them again, and learns a fresh conclusion; and so goes on multiplying itself *ad infinitum*.

Fifth, the *transcendental prophetic spirit*. This is the property of prophets and some saints. By it the unseen tables and statutes of the Law are revealed from the other world, together with several of the sciences of the Realms Celestial and Terrestrial, and pre-eminently theology, the science of Deity, which the intelligential and discursive spirit cannot compass. It is this that is alluded to in the text, "*Thus did We inspire thee with a spirit from Our power. Thou didst not know what is the Book, nor what is Faith,* [41] *but we made that spirit a light wherewith we guide whom We will of our vassals. And thou, verily, dost guide into a straight way*".[1] And here, a word to thee, thou recluse in thy

[1] S. 42, 52.

143

rational world of the intelligence! Why should it be impossible that beyond reason there should be a further plane, on which appear things which do not appear on the plane of the intelligence, just as it is possible for the intelligence itself to be a plane above the discriminating faculty and the senses; and for revelations of wonders and marvels to be made to it that were beyond the reach of the senses and the discriminative faculty? Beware of making the ultimate perfection stop at thyself! Consider the intuitive faculty of poetry, if thou wilt have an example of everyday experience, taken from those special gifts which particularize some men. Behold how this gift, which is a sort of perceptive faculty, is the exclusive possession of some; while it is so completely denied to others that they cannot even distinguish the scansion of a typical measure from that of its several variations. Mark how extraordinary is this intuitive faculty in some others, insomuch that they produce music and melodies, and all the various grief-, delight-, slumber-, weeping-, madness-, murder-, and swoon-producing modes! Now these effects only occur strongly in one who has this original, intuitive sense. A person destitute of it hears the sounds just as much as the other, but the emotional effects are by him only very faintly experienced, and he exhibits surprise at those whom they send into raptures or swoons. And even were all the professors of music in the world to call a conference with a view of making him understand the meaning of this musical sense, they would be quite powerless to do so. Here, then, is an example taken from the gross phenomena which are easiest for you to understand. Apply this now to this peculiar prophetical sense. And strive earnestly to become one of those who experience mystically something [42] of the prophetic spirit; for *saints* have a specially large portion thereof. If thou canst not compass this, then try, by the discipline of the syllogisms and analogies set forth or alluded to in a previous page, to be one of those who have knowledge of it scientifically. But if this, too, is beyond thy powers, then the least thou canst do is to become one of those who simply have faith in it ("*Allāh exalts those that have faith among you, and those who acquire knowledge, in their several ranks*").[1] Scientific knowledge is above faith, and mystic experience is above knowledge. The province of mystic experience is feeling; of knowledge, ratiocination; and of faith, bare acceptance of the creed of one's fathers, together with an unsuspicious attitude towards the two superior classes.

You now know the five human spirits. So we proceed: they are all of them *Lights*, for it is through their agency that every sort of existing thing is manifested, including objects of sense and imagination. For though it is true that the lower animals also perceive these said objects, mankind possesses a different, more refined, and higher species of those two faculties, they having been created in man for a different, higher, and more noble end. In the lower animals they were only created as an instrument for acquiring food, and for subjecting them to mankind. But in mankind they were created to be a net to chase a noble quarry through all the present world; to wit, the first-principles of the religious sciences. For example, a man may, in perceiving with his visual sense a certain individual, apprehend, through his intelligence, a universal and absolute idea, as we saw in our example of Abdul-Raḥmān the son of 'Awf.

PART III. — THE APPLICATION TO THE LIGHT-VERSE AND THE VEILS TRADITION

(*i*) THE EXPOSITION OF THE SYMBOLISM OF THE LIGHT-VERSE

We now come to what the symbolism of this Verse actually signifies. The full exposition of the parallelism between these five classes of Spirit, and the fivefold Niche, Glass, Lamp, Tree, and Oil, [43] could be indefinitely prolonged. But we must be content with shortly indicating the method of this symbolism.

[1] S. 58, 11.

1. Consider *the sensory spirit*. Its lights, you observe, come through several apertures, the eyes, ears, nostrils, etc. Now the aptest symbol for this, in our world of experience, is the *Niche* for a lamp in a wall.

2. Take next *the imaginative spirit*. It has three peculiarities: first, that it is of the stuff that this gross lower world is made of, for its objects have definite and limited size, and shape, and dimension, and are definitely related to the subject in respect of distance. Further, one of the properties of a gross substance whereof corporal attributes are predicated is to be opaque to the light of pure intelligence, which transcends these categories of direction, quantity, and distance. But, secondly, if that substance is clarified, refined, disciplined, and controlled, it attains to a correspondence with and a similarity to the ideas of the intelligence, and becomes transparent to light from them. Thirdly, the imagination is at first very much needed, in order that intelligential knowledge may be controlled by it, so that the knowledge be not disturbed, unsettled, and dissipated, and so get out of hand. The images supplied by the imagination hold together the knowledge supplied by the intellect. Now, in the world of everyday experience the sole object in which you will find these three peculiarities, in relation to physical light, is *Glass*. For glass also is originally an opaque substance, but is clarified and refined until it becomes transparent to the light of a lamp, which indeed it transmits unaltered. Again, glass keeps the lamp from being put out by a draught or violent jerking. [44] By what, then, could possibly the imagination be more aptly symbolized?

3. *The intelligential spirit*, which gives cognizance of the divine ideas. The point of the symbolism must be obvious to you. You know it already from our preceding explanation of the doctrine that the prophets are a *"light-giving lamp"*.

4. *The ratiocinative spirit*. Its peculiarity is to begin from one proposition, then to branch out into two, which two

become four and so on, until by this process of logical division they become very numerous. It leads, finally, to conclusions which in their turn become germs producing like conclusions, these latter being also susceptible of continuation, each with each. The symbol which our world yields for this is a *Tree*. And when further we consider that the fruit of the discursive reason is material for this multiplying, establishing, and fixing of all knowledge, it will naturally not be typified by trees like quince, apple, pomegranate, nor, in brief, by any other tree whatever, except the *Olive*. For the quintessence of the fruit of the olive is its oil, which is the material which feeds the lamps, and has this peculiarity, as against all other oils, that it increases radiance. Again, if people give the adjective "blessed" to specially fruitful trees, surely the tree the fruitfulness whereof is absolutely infinite should be named *Blessed*! Finally, if the ramifications of those pure intellectual propositions do not admit of relation to direction and to distance, them may the anti-typical tree well be said to be *"Neither from the East nor from the West"*.

5. *The transcendental prophetic spirit*, which is possessed by saints as well as prophets if it is absolutely luminous and clear. For the thought-spirit is divided [45] into that which needs be instructed, advised, and supplied from without, if the acquisition of knowledge is to be continuous; while a portion of it is absolutely clear, as though it were self-luminous, and had no external source of supply. Applying these considerations, we see how justly this clear, strong natural faculty is described by the words, *"Whose Oil were well-night luminant, though Fire touched it not"*; for there be Saints whose light shines so bright that it is "well-nigh" independent of that which Prophets supply, while there be Prophets whose light is "well-nigh" independent of that which Angels supply. Such is the symbolism, and aptly does it typify this class.

And inasmuch as the lights of the human spirit are graded rank on rank, then that of Sense comes first, the foundation and preparation for the Imagination (for the latter can only be conceived as superimposed after Sense); those of the Intelligence and Discursive Reason come thereafter. All which explains why the Glass is, as it were, the place for the Lamp's immanence; and the Niche, for the Glass: that is to say, the Lamp is within the Glass, and the Glass within the Niche. Finally, the existence, as we have seen, of a graded succession of Lights explains the words of the text "*Light upon Light*".

Epilogue: the Darkness-Verse

But this symbolism holds only for the hearts of true believers, or of prophets and saints, but not for the hearts of misbelievers; for the term "light" is expressive of right-guidance alone. But as for the man who is turned from the path of guidance, he is false, he is darkness; nay, he is darker than darkness. For darkness is neutral; it leads one neither one way nor the other; but the minds of mis-believers, and the whole of their perceptions, are perverse, and support each other mutually in the actual deluding of their owners. They are like a man "*in some fathomless sea, overwhelmed* [46] *by billow topped by billow topped by cloud; darkness on darkness piled!*"[1] Now that fathomless sea is the World, this world of mortal dangers, of evil chances, of blinding trouble. The first "billow" is the wave of lust, whereby souls acquire the bestial attributes,[2] and are occupied with sensual pleasures, and the satisfaction of worldly ambitions, so that "*they eat and luxuriate like cattle. Hell shall be their place of entertainment!*"[3] Well does this wave represent darkness, therefore; since love for the creature makes the soul both blind and deaf. The second "billow" is the wave of the ferocious attributes, which impel the soul to wrath, enmity, hatred, prejudice, envy, boastfulness, ostenta-

[1] S. 24, 40.

[2] The following tripartite division of the soul, with its analogues, is Platonic (see *Republic*, bk. iv).

[3] S. 12, 47.

148

tion, pride. Well is this, too, the symbol of darkness, for wrath is the demon of man's intelligence; and well also is it the uppermost billow, for anger is mostly stronger even than lust; swelling wrath diverts the soul from lust and makes it oblivious of enjoyment; lust cannot for a moment stand up against anger at its height. Finally, "the cloud" is rank beliefs, and lying heresies, and corrupt imaginings, which become so many veils veiling the misbeliever from the true faith, from knowledge of the Real, and from illumination by the sunlight of the Koran and human intelligence. For it is the property of a cloud to veil the shining of the sunlight. Now these things, being all of them darkness, are well called "*darkness on darkness piled*", shutting the soul out from the knowledge of things near, [47] let alone things far away; veiling the misbeliever, therefore, from the apprehension of the miraculousness of the Prophet, though he is so near to grasp, so manifest upon the least reflection. Truly it might be said of such an one that "*when a man putteth forth his hand, he can well-nigh see it not*".[1] Finally, if all these Lights have, as we saw, their source and origin in the great Primary, the One Real, then every Confessor of the Unity may well believe that "*the man for whom Allāh doth not cause light, no light at all hath he*".[1]

And now you must be content with thus much of the mysteries of this Verse.

(*ii*) THE EXPOSITION OF THE SYMBOLISM OF THE SEVENTY THOUSAND VEILS

What is the signification of the tradition, "*Allāh hath Seventy Thousand Veils of Light and Darkness: were He to withdraw their curtain, then would the splendours of His Aspect surely consume everyone who apprehended Him with his sight*". (Some read "seven hundred veils"; others, "seventy thousand".)

I explain it thus. Allāh is in, by, and for himself glorious. A veil is necessarily related to those from whom

[1] S. 24, 40.

the glorious object is veiled. Now these among men are of three kinds, according as their veils are pure darkness; mixed darkness and light; or pure light. The subdivisions of these three are very numerous. That much only is certain. I could no doubt make some far-fetched enumeration of these subdivisions; but I have no confidence in the results of such defining and enumerating, for none knows whether they were really intended or not. As for the fixing of the number at seven hundred, or at seventy thousand, this is a matter that only the prophetic power can compass. My own clear impression, however, is that these numbers are not mentioned in the way of definite enumeration at all, for [48] numbers are not infrequently mentioned without any intention of limitation, but rather to denote some indefinitely great quantity: God knows best! That point, then, is beyond our competence, and all I can do now is to unfold to you these three main divisions and a few of the subdivisions.

1. Those veiled by Pure Darkness

The first division consists of those who are veiled by pure darkness. These are the atheists *"who believe not in Allāh, nor the Last Day"*.[1] These are they *"who love this present life more than that which is to come"*,[2] for they do not believe in that which is to come at all. They fall into subdivisions.

First, there are those who desire to discover a cause to account for the world, and make Nature that cause. But nature is an attribute which inheres in material substances, and is immanent in them, and is moreover a dark one, for it has no knowledge, nor perception, nor self-consciousness, nor consciousness, nor light perceived through the medium of physical sight.

Secondly, there are those whose preoccupation is self, and who in no wise busy themselves about the quest for causality. Rather, they live the life of the beasts of the field. This veil is, as it were, their self-centred ego, and their lusts of darkness; for there is no darkness so intense

[1] S. 4, 37.   [2] S. 14, 3.

as slavery to self-impulse and self-love. "*Hast thou seen*", saith Allāh, "*the man who makes self-impulse his god?*"[1] and the Prophet, "*Self-impulse is the hatefullest of the gods worshippped instead of Allāh*".

This last division may further be subdivided. There is one class which has thought that this world's Chief End is the satisfaction of one's wants, lusts, and animal pleasures, whether connected with sex, or food, or drink, or raiment. Thcsc, therefore, are the creatures of pleasure; pleasure is their god, the goal of their ambition, and in winning her they believe that they have won felicity. Deliberately and willingly do they place themselves at the level of the beasts of the field; nay, at a viler level than the beasts. Can darkness be conceived more intense than this? Such men are, indeed, veiled by darkness unadulterated. Another class has thought that man's Chief End is conquest and domination — the taking of prisoners, and captives, and life. [49] Such is the idea of the Arabs, certain of the Kurds, and withal very numerous fools. Their veil is the dark veil of the ferocious attributes, because these dominate them, so that they deem the running down of their quarry the height of bliss. These, then, are content to occupy the level of beasts of prey, ay, one more degraded still. A third class has supposed that the Chief End is riches and prosperity, because wealth is the instrument for the satisfaction of every lust. Their concern is therefore the heaping up and multiplication of riches — the multi-plication of property, real estate, personal estate, thoroughbreds, flocks, herds, fields, and the rest. Such men hoard their pelf underground — you may see them toiling their lives long, embarking on perils by land, perils by sea, up-dale, down-lea, piling up wealth, and yet grudging it to themselves — and how much more others! These are they whom the Prophet had in view when he said, "*Poor wretch, the slave of money! Poor wretch, the slave of gold!*" And, indeed, what darkness is intenser

---

[1] S. 25, 43.

than that which blinds mankind to the fact that gold and silver are just two metals, unwanted for their own sakes, no better than gravel unless they are made a means to various ends, and spent upon things worth spending on? A fourth class has advanced a step higher than the total folly of these last, and has supposed that the supreme felicity is found in the extension of a man's personal reputation, the spread of his own renown, the increase of his own following and his influence over others. You may see these admiring themselves in their own looking-glasses! One of them, who may be suffering hunger and penury at home, will be spending his substance on clothes, and trying to look his smartest therein, [50] just in order to avoid contemptuous glances when he walks abroad!

Innumerable are the varieties of this species, and one and all are veiled from Allāh by pure darkness, and they themselves are darkness. So there is no need to mention all the individual varieties, when once attention has been called to the species. One of these varieties which we should, however, mention is the sort that confesses with their tongues the Creed "There is no god but Allāh", but are probably urged thereto by fear alone, or the desire to beg from Mohammedans, or to curry favour with them, or to get financial assistance out of them, or, by a merely fanatical zeal, to support the opinions of their fathers. For if the Creed fails to impel these to good works, by no means shall it secure their elevation from the dark sphere to light. Rather are their patron-saints devils, who lead them from the light nto the darkness. But he whom the Creed so touches that his evil deeds displease him and his good deeds give him pleasure, has passed from pure darkness even though he be a great sinner still.

2. Those veiled by mixed Light and Darkness

The second division consists of those who are veiled by mixed light and darkness. It consists of three main kinds: first, those whose darkness has its origin in the Senses;

secondly, in the Imagination; thirdly, in false syllogisms of the Intelligence.

First, then, those veiled by the darkness *of the Senses*. These are persons who one and all have got beyond that self-absorption which was the characteristic of all the first division, as they deify something outside the self, and have some yearning for the knowledge of the Deity. The first grade of these consists of the idol-worshippers, the last grade consists of the dualists; between which extremes come other grades.

The first, the idolaters, are aware, in general, that they have a deity whom they must prefer to their dark selves, and believe [51] that their deity is mightier than everything else, and more to be prized than every prize. But the darkness of sense veils from them the knowledge that they must transcend the world of sense in this quest; so that they make for themselves from the more precious minerals, gold, silver, gems, etc., figures splendidly fashioned, and then take these images unto themselves as gods. Such men are veiled by the light of Majesty and Beauty from the attributes of Allāh and his light; they have affixed these attributes to sense-perceived bodies; which sense has blocked out the light of Allāh; for the senses are darkness in relation to the World Spiritual, as we have already shown.

The second class, composed of the remotest Turkish tribes, who have no organized religious community and no definite religious code, believe that they have a deity, and that that deity is some particularly beautiful object; so that when they see a human being of exceptional beauty, or similarly a tree, or a horse, etc., they worship it and call it their god. These are veiled by the light of Beauty mixed with the darkness of Sense. They have penetrated further than the idolaters into the Realm of Light in the discovery of Light, for they are worshippers of Beauty in the absolute, not in the individual; and they do not limit it specially to one individual to the exclusion of others; and then, again, the Beauty they worship is of Nature's hand, and not of their own.

The third class say, Our deity must be in His essence Light, glorious in His express image, majestic in Himself, terrible in His presence, intolerant of approach; and yet He must be likewise perceptible. For the imperceptible is meaningless in the opinion of these. Then because they find Fire thus characterized, they worship it and take it unto themselves as lord. Such are veiled by the light of Dominion and of Glory, [52] which are, indeed, two of the Lights of Allāh.

The fourth class think that, since we have control over fire, kindling or quenching it at will, it cannot serve as divinity. Only that which possessing the attribute of Dominion and Glory and has us under its absolute sway, and is withal very high and lifted up — only this avails for divinity. Astrology is the science that is celebrated among this folk, the attribution to each star of its special influence; so that some worship Cynosura and others Jupiter, and others some other heavenly body, according to the many influences with which they believe the several stars are endued. These, then, are veiled by Light, the Light of the Sublime, the Luminous, the Potent; which are also three of the Lights of Allāh.

The fifth class support the fourth in their fundamental idea, but they say that it does not befit their Lord to be describable as small or great among light-giving substances, but He must be the greatest of them; and so they worship the Sun, which, they say, is the Greatest of All. Such are veiled by the Light of Greatness, in addition to the former lights; but are still blent with the darkness of the Senses.

The sixth class advance higher still and say, The sun has no monopoly of light; bodies other than the sun have each one its light. So, as the deity must have no partner in lightfulness, they worship Absolute Light, which embraces all lights, and think that It is the Lord of the Universe, and that all good things are attributable to it. Then, since they perceive the existence of evils in the world, and will by no means allow them to be attributed to their deity. He being wholly void of evil, they conceive of a struggle between Him and the Darkness, [53] and these two are called by them, as I suppose, Yazdān and Ahrimān; which is the sect of the Dualists.

This must suffice for the exemplification of this division, the classes whereof are more numerous than those we have mentioned.

Second, those veiled by some light, mixed with the darkness of *the Imagination*. These have got beyond the senses, for they assert the existence of something behind the objects of sense, but are unable to get beyond the imagination, and so have worshipped a Being who actually sits on a throne. The meanest grade of these is called the Corporealists; then all the varius Karrāmites, into whose writings and opinions we cannot go here, for to multiply words thereon were bootless. But the highest in degree are those who denied to Allāh corporality and all its accidentia, except one — *direction*, and that *direction upwards*; for (say they) that which is not referable to any direction, and cannot be characterized as either within or without the world, does not exist at all, since it cannot be imagined by the imagination.[1] They failed to perceive that the very first degree of the intelligibilia takes us clean beyond all reference whatsoever to direction and dimension.

Third, those who are veiled by Light divine, mixed with the darkness of false syllogisms of *the Intelligence*, and who worship a deity that "Heareth, Seeth, and hath Knowledge, Power, Will, Life", and transcends all direction, including direction upwards; but whose conception of these attributes is relative to their own; so that some of them may even have declared outright that His "speech" is with sounds and letters like ours; while others advanced a step higher, it may be, and said, "Nay, but it is like our thought-speech, both soundless and letterless". Thus, when they were challenged to show that "hearing, sight, life", etc., are *real* in Allāh they fell back on what was essentially anthropomorphism, though they

[1] See Averroes, opusc. cit., p. 61, Cairo ed., p. 51.

repudiated it formally; for they utterly failed to apprehend what [54] the attribution of these ideas to Allāh really signifies. Thus they say, in regard to His will, that it is contingent, like ours; that it is a demanding and a purposing, like ours. All of which opinions are well known, and we need not go into further details with regard to them. These, then, are veiled by several of the divine Lights, mixed with the darkness of false syllogisms of the intelligence. All such are various classes of the second division, which consists of those veiled by mixed light and darkness.

3. Those veiled by Pure Light

The third division are those veiled with pure Light, and they also fall into several classes. I cannot enumerate all, but only refer to three.

The *first* of these have searched out and understood the true meaning of the divine attributes, and have grasped that when the divine attributes are named Speech, Will, Power, Knowledge, and the rest, it is not according to our human mode of nomenclature. And this has led them to avoid denoting Him by these attributes altogether, and to denote Him simply by a reference to His creation, as Moses did in his answer to Pharaoh, when the latter asked, "*And what, pray, is the Lord of the Universe?*" and he replied, "'*The Lord, Whose Holiness transcends even the ideas of these attributes*', He, the Mover and Orderer of the Heavens".[1]

The *second* mount higher than these, inasmuch as they perceived that the Heavens are a plurality, and that the mover of every several Heaven is another being, called an Angel, and that these angels form a plurality, and that their relation to the other Lights Divine is as the relation of the stars to all other visible lights.[2] Then they perceived that these Heavens are enveloped by another Sphere, by whose motion all the rest revolve once in twenty-four hours, and that finally The LORD is He Who communicates motion to this outermost Sphere, which

[1] See S. 26, 23 ff.   [2] Cf. S. 41, 11.

encloses all the rest, on the ground (say they) that plurality must be denied of Him.

The *third* mount higher than these also, [55] and say that this direct communication of motion to the celestial bodies must be an act of service to the Lord of the Universe, an act of worship and obedience to His command, and rendered by one of His creatures, an Angel, who stands to the pure Light Divine in the relation of the Moon to the other visible lights; and they asserted that the LORD is the Obeyed-One of this Angelic Movent, and that the Almighty must be considered the universal Movent indirectly and by way of command only (*amr*),[1] but not directly by way of act. The explication of which "command" and what it really is contains much that is obscure, and too difficult for most minds, besides being beyond the scope of this book.

These, then, are grades all of which are veiled by Lights without admixture of Darkness.

4. The Goal of the Quest

But those who ATTAIN make a fourth grade, to Whom, in turn, it has been made clear that this Obeyed-One, if identified with Allāh, would have been given attributes negative of His pure Unity and perfection, on account of a mystery which it is not in the scope of this book to reveal; and that the relation of this Obeyed-One to THE REAL EXISTENCE is as the relaxation of the Sun to Essential Light, or of the live coal to the Elemental Fire; and so "turned their faces"[2] from him who moves the heavens and him who issued the command (*amara*) for their moving, and Attained unto an Existent who transcends ALL that is comprehensible by human Sight or human Insight; for they found IT transcendent of and separate from every characterization that in the foregoing we have made.

And these last are also divided. For one class the whole content of the perceptible is consumed away — con-

[1] See S. 7, 53.   [2] See M., pp. [30, 31].

sumed, obliterated, and annihilated; yet the soul itself remains contemplating the absolute Beauty and Holiness, and contemplating herself in her beauty, which is conferred on her by this Attainment unto the Presence Divine. [56] In them, then, the seen things, but not the seeing soul, are obliterated.

And they are passed by others, among whom are the Few of the Few; whom "the splendours of the Countenance sublime consume",[1] and the majesty of the Divine Glory obliterate; so that they are themselves blotted out, annihilated. For self-contemplation there is no more found a place, because with the self they have no longer anything to do. Nothing remaineth any more save the One, the Real; and the import of His word, *"All perisheth save His Countenance"*,[2] becomes the experience of the soul. To this we have made reference in the first chapter, where we set forth in what sense they named this state "Identity", and how they conceived the same.

Such is the ultimate degree of those who Attain. Some of these souls had not, in their upward Progress and Ascent, to climb step by step the stages we have described; neither did their ascension cost them any length of time; but with their first flight they attained to the knowledge of the Holiness and the confession that His sovereignty transcends everything that it must be confessed to transcend. They were overcome at the very first by the knowledge which overcame the rest at the very last. The onset of God's epiphany came upon them with one rush, so that all that is apprehensible by the sight of Sense or by the insight of Intelligence was by "the splendours of His Countenance utterly consumed". It may be that that first was the way of Abraham, the Friend of Allāh, while the latter was the way of Mohammed, the Beloved of Allāh. Allāh alone knoweth the mysteries of their Progress and of their Stations on the Way of Light.

[1] See the Tradition on p. [2].
[2] S. 28, 88.

Such is our account of the classes of the veiled by the Veils; and it were not strange if, after all these Stations were fully classified and the veils of the Pilgrims Mystical were fully studied, the number of classes were found to amount to Seventy Thousand. Yet, if you look carefully, you shall find that of them all not one falls outside the divisions which we have set forth. For, as we have shown, they must be veiled by their own human attributes; *or* by the senses, imagination, discursive intelligence; *or* by pure light.

This is what has occurred to me by way of answer [57] to your interrogations, though these came to me at a time when my thought was divided, and my mind preoccupied, and my attention given to other matters than this. May not my suggestion be, then, that you ask forgiveness for me for anything wherein my pen has erred, or my foot has slipped? For 'tis a hazardous thing to plunge into the fathomless sea of the divine mysteries; and hard, hard it is to essay the discovery of the Lights Supernal that are beyond the Veil.

———————

III
THE WAY OF THE SEEKER

FOREWORD

This English version of Hakim Sanai's *Sair ul Ibad ilal Maad* is offered in the same spirit as my previous work on Sanai.* The same general comments and caveats which I made there apply here also, so I shall not repeat them in detail. But, as before, I must begin by placing on record my debt and gratitude to a scholar whose labours and insights were of invaluable assistance to me in tackling this present work.

I am referring to Dr. Sayed B. Majrouh, whom I had the honour to meet at a seminar held in Kabul to mark the nine-hundredth anniversary of Sanai's birth, and in whom I was delighted to recognize a kindred approach to Sufi studies. For the seminar Dr. Majrouh had published a most interesting paper on Sanai's *Sair ul Ibad*, to which he appended an abridged translation in French.** This stimulated me to make a detailed study of the Persian text, with a view to producing a version in English.

This present translation, therefore, owes much to that of Dr. Majrouh; though I have made numerous important alterations and additions from my own reading of the original. I have also gone even further than Dr. Majrouh in eliminating the seemingly extraneous and often misleading titles and subtitles, which were interpolated into the Persian text at a later date. What few titles remain are my own.

Sair ul Ibad was written around the year 1111 A.D., that is to say about twenty years prior to Sanai's masterwork, *The Walled Garden of Truth*. It comprises about eight hundred couplets, and of these the final third, a traditional panegyric, has not been reproduced here. It is dedicated to Mohammed ben Mansur, the Qadi of Sarakhs, and identifies him as the 'man of light' referred to at the end of the main poem.

---

* Hakim Sanai: *The Walled Garden of Truth*, translated and abridged by David Pendlebury, London 1974; New York 1976.
**First published in *Afghanistan Magazine*, Vol. 30 No. 2.

PROLOGUE

Now welcome, kingly messenger!
You with the waves for your throne,
you with fire for your crown!
You are not of water,
yet stir it into movement;
you are not of earth,
yet you lend it shape.
You are at once the outwardness
and inwardness of gardens:
the nurse and the bridegroom of branches.
In good times and in bad,
you drive along both cloud and craft.
Through the energy born of matter
the rhythm of animal breath
is linked to you.
Because of you, fire shines
like a mass of coral;
and water gleams
like foaming emerald.
For all your lowly nature,
you resemble the spirit:
for you are unseen, and yet you are.
In this, our tomb of earth,
our coffin of fire,
it is from you
the soul draws strength and substance.

How long, angelic one, will you tie yourself
to the baseness of this base world?
With one bound, throw off
the bonds that bind you
to fire and water.
Come near awhile,
and hear from my visionary tongue
the riddle of my creation:
thus you will see
it is not only the wind
that has never been tamed!

I. BIRTH

When, in the expanse of the ancient abode, from out of being my existence was poured, from those lofty summits I descended into this lowly world. Here I found a nurse, as old as the movement of the stars. It was this fertile old woman, oblivious both to sun and shade, who suckled and reared the human race. Possessing the primeval seed, she gave birth to plants and animals, and fed each species according to its rank.

Like a mother, she reared me at her breast. I was a child; and yet in her eyes I was just like a piece of wood. For my part I was unconscious of my state: I fed on plants, and lived with plants. My nurse made me go through all kinds of existence. First she made me a robe of green; then she gave me a mantle of ruby red. When I cast off red and green, she sewed me a coat of white. Then, when I tore my white coat, she clothed me once more in red.

Meanwhile, on a plot of dark earth, she was quietly building a pure white chamber for me, full of seven-headed monsters. It was a chamber with six sides, four compartments and five doors. She furnished the interior of this chamber and covered it on the outside. Then, for my development, she showed me for nine months through nine spheres. When my constitution had become strong and solid, she sent me away to the town of my father.

On the borders of Rome and Ethiopia I found a city surrounded by beautiful flames. On the outside it was new, and on the inside it was old. It had an attractive soil and an evil-smelling atmosphere. Everything growing there was upside-down, like a reflection in water. Like the heart of a scholar, it had branches pointing downwards and roots pointing upwards. In that region they had pitched tents of wind and earth with pegs of fire and ropes of water.

There was an angel there with two faces and ten heads, the offspring of two mothers and two fathers. He was the essence of nobility and prodigality, knowledge and justice; but his was the pen that wrote greed, hatred and desire. He was the force animating the souls of demons and beasts, both wild and tame. It was from him that matter received its power; and it was he, too, who activated the intelligence and the organs of sense. His exterior was made of fire, his inward reality of light. Externally he was one; internally he was divided into four. His strength lay in the enduring balance of mother and father, matter and essence; and his weakness lay in the frailty of their union and the transience of their offspring.

And so, through my faculties I became acquainted with the Lord of creation and corruption. He received me kindly and gave me substance; he developed my soul and fitted out my dwelling place. When he enumerated the gates and boundaries of the house, he saw fit to entrust the four boundaries to seven patient bearers, and the five gates to five seekers of knowledge.

From the moment I awoke to the tangible reality of my existence, I began at once to eat like a beast. Then I saw herds of wild animals and demons. Although melancholy by nature, they were in a state of blissful satiation. I crossed mountains and deserts, and yet wherever I went I was overwhelmingly depressed by those beasts with huge appetites and short sight. Truly in that place I had my fill of the sight of those insatiably hungering creatures.

There is in the soul an intuition of a superior state; and the moment that this showed itself, it instantly wrenched me aloft, and I leaped from the safety of the earth into the skies.

However, when I returned to my natural state, I was once more among demons and all kinds of beasts. My physical nature was pulling me downwards, while my creative essence was pushing me upwards. And there I remained, suspended, my goal far off, the way arduous and full of fearsome dangers. I stayed there, confounded, without knowledge or strength, with no other guides than the blind beasts.

Finally I turned my back on those pastures and that path; and then I found another path — and a guide — with whom I fell in love.

II. THE GUIDE

One day, at the end of a narrow road, I saw someone in the shadows. It was an old man, gentle and serene, modest and subtle, at once slow moving and agile. Though of the earth, he was faster than time; though old, he was younger than the first signs of spring. Eagerly I spoke to him:

— Light of my nights!
Healing saviour of my fevers!
You who are so noble, subtle and blithe,
from where do you have such perfect beauty?

— I am beyond both substance and place.
My father is the Almighty's agent,
first outcome of eternity,
first sun to dawn from nothingness;
his throne is innocent of blemish,
his carpet is not from the loom
of heaven and earth;
in the house of non-existence,
it is he who weaves
the fabric of eternal existence.

I remain here at his command
on this earth here below,
breathing this malodorous air:
it is not out of ignorance
that I stay within this useless world,
but in keeping with a lofty purpose.

But you, who have such noble origins,
how can you have sunk to such depths?
A prince, the peer of Gabriel,
stringing along with dogs and flies!

— But what profit is there
in any of this?

— We shall see what profit there will be.
Does a donkey know the destiny of Jesus?
Can a deaf man hear the song of David?
I am a jewel lying in the dust;
I am Joseph hidden in the well.

He poured out these subtleties and a thousand more like them, until I had to beg him to cut short his discourse.

> — These conceits are on your account,
> since words and speech are the way of your world;
> words are from the kingdom of ignorance:
> in the bosom of knowledge they have no use.
>
> So leave this room full of bones to the dogs,
> and set out for the eternal city;
> leave behind your vegetable nature,
> and you can become a soaring angel;
> take wisdom by the hand,
> and spurn the nourishment of beasts.
>
> For your journey on this arduous path,
> your only provision will be fire:
> not the fire of helplessness,
> but the fire which is the source of life.
>
> If you have eyes to see,
> I will be your friend;
> if you have feet for travelling,
> I will take your hand.

I became receptive to his discerning wisdom. I made my heart his dwelling place, and my body his steed, Buraq. He became my sight and I became his feet; and we both decided to undertake the voyage.

———————

III. THE JOURNEY

On the first day our way led to a heap of earth which stank of putrefaction, and which was composed half of water and half of fire. There I saw a mean and gloomy city.

Rampaging wolves brazenly wandered about. Rats, the size of cats, ate their young there; and there were snakes there, the size of pigs. Sometimes demons bestrode these beasts; sometimes scorpions tended the snakes. Packs of dogs dwelt there, devouring carrion and rotting entrails.

The inhabitants of this region gave birth to demons, and then screamed with terror at the sight of their own creations. They were at constant war with their own shadows, so that the sight of the sun and moon was an affliction to them.

I saw there a huge and venomous serpent, which had one head, seven faces and four mouths. With every breath it took it swallowed whatever it found around it. I asked my guide what it was.

— That serpent is the ancient angel of death,
the devourer of desert caravans.
This road you see is empty
because of the terror he inspires.
Were it not for me,
should he seize you, that would be
the last you saw of the light of day:
he would transform you
into a hideous creature like himself,
an essence of smoke and fire;
he would sever your seven limbs
and consign them to the elements;
and your four component elements
would be scattered over the seven planets.

But since I am at your side,
there is nothing to fear:
a single flashing glance from me
is a hundred times more terrible than his.
My glance is the emerald which blinds him.

So saying, my guide turned towards the dragon. When it saw us it came crawling towards us and lay down at our feet like a dog. Then it began to sweep our path before us with its tail.

We left that region and travelled on till we reached a valley. It was inhabited by innumerable demons, whose eyes were in their necks and whose tongues were in their hearts.

After leaving this baleful tribe, we reached another place, a rocky desert, where the people were blackened by infernal smoke. A race of static beings — like the minds of the ignorant — bewildered, and with eyes only for each other. They were full of wind like bagpipes, and like them had three necks and two mouths. I saw apes running by, with cats' heads and dogs' tails. I glimpsed beings, whose heads, like a narcissus, were formed into a single eye, and whose bodies had innumerable arms and hands, like a plane tree.

At last I came to a mountain and, in order to cross it, I reduced my body to a slender reed. I was tired from journeying and from all that I had seen. The comb was new, but the hair had grown grey.

Then after crossing a desert, with many a sigh, we finally arrived on the shore of an immense sea. I was petrified by the fear of drowning in those swirling waters. My companion reassured me, saying:

> — Take courage and enter!
> You are prey to evil delusions:
> in the three stages now ahead,
> three evil spirits will dog your steps;
> unless you wish to founder in the depths,
> you must chain up these earthly demons;
> unless indeed your wish is to be drowned,
> leave all that belongs to this place behind.
> Once you are purified of this dross,
> your feet themselves will be your ship.

When my guide had imparted this secret to me, I entered a place where I saw a world full of youth. Its inhabitants were all mad, but none among them was mad with love. They were all in chains, and yet these chains could not be seen. They were all ignorant — like mice oblivious of the falcon. All of them were drunk, swaying like branches in the wind. Their paws were dirty, their brains a tangled muddle. All of them were sick and idle; carrying loads, but without any real burden on their backs. All were perplexed, but lacking any desire to know. All were motionless, but not out of any spirit of patience. They were all open-mouthed, like oysters; with their heads withdrawn, like tortoises. Their hearts were the seat of unreality. They were like hares, who sleep open-eyed and seem to be awake. And yet, despite all their excesses, these creatures had the capacity to receive mystical illumination.

In this world I also encountered sea monsters, tall as mountains, slayers of the wise and enslavers of the just. On the orders of the lord of these regions, they fed on angels and demons. Through all of this the old man was my guide and companion, and I was his vehicle.

When we had traversed this watery way, we suddenly had to stop. For, to our dismay, our tent no longer had any ropes: we no longer had the support either of earth or of water. I protested to my guide that I was afraid of rising into the air without wings.

> — Your straightforwardness of thinking
> is the product of these watery regions;
> the distortion in your thought, likewise,
> has its origin here:
> just as an arrow, soaked in water,
> bends and turns into a bow,
> thus a man bends and turns coward.
>
> Reunite these disparate elements
> in the totality they come from!
> Be straight as an arrow
> taut in a bow!
> When your opinion
> becomes a straight certitude,
> you'll be like an arrow
> with wings at your feet.

I obeyed his instructions. We left that place and rose up towards the heights. As we did so, I asked him whose region it was that we were travelling through.

— His who is messenger of the King.
Like water, his nature is both moist and cold,
but he is more mobile yet than fire:
one moment he diminishes,
only to increase himself the next;
and now, since he it is who here holds sway,
his realm surrounds us on all sides.

In the course of our journey I saw in the distance a castle on a green island. It was built of fire and water; and within it there were magicians, conjurors of forms. These creatures had the heads of dragons, the tails of fish and human trunks. Their heads were as strong as an animal's, but their feet were weak and frail like an ant's.

Through magic powers they forged new forms from old objects and made evil appear in the guise of good. One made a garden out of a pile of rubbish; another transformed a crow into a pheasant.

I found myself looking at a world where egoism was nurtured and enshrined. Gold and silver were worshipped like gods.

In this enchanted castle I also saw a large pool built of stone, in which there was a monster with seven throats and six teeth. Its head was turned towards the waters of lust, and its tail towards the fires of passion. Its breath generated the power of the animal spirit, and its tail was the snare of bestial existence. Whatever fell into its trap was driven by its breath towards its tail. It ate ravenously and incessantly, and never closed its jaws for a second. At every moment it opened them wider and stretched its tail even higher.

Truly, when I perceived this devouring maw, I was gripped with such terror that my face went pale, my body trembled and my strength left me. The monster started to come for me, but my companion ordered me to step on its head.

— Although its nature is in essence evil,
here it will serve you as a boat:
tread on its head, and you will win the day!
Close its jaws with your foot and trap its tongue!

I took refuge and comfort in his words, and my fear vanished. I trod on the monster's head, and asked my guide what manner of dire killer this was.

— A hunter from the lord of hell.
Dwellers in the ether are in its debt,
and it prospers the guardians of hellfire;
strangest of all, this den, from end to end,
is the resort of devout ascetics,
for they are such because of this beast;
for though of like nature with the animal soul
is also underlies man's spiritual power.

After my guide had told me this, we left the monster and suddenly saw a narrow valley.

It was a valley of terror. Scorpions and serpents moved about among mountains of fire. It was inhabited by sorcerers who conjured up demons. They were drunk with boiling water and pitch, and held spears and swords of flame in their hands. They destroyed all fair forms and blackened the face of everything beautiful. One moment they transformed fairies into wicked jinns; the next they howled like demons themselves.

And then, ahead of us there was a mountain of flames and smoke, which looked like a sphere cleft in two halves. At its feet I saw nothing but bottomless abysses and yawning chasms; and on its crests, which rose as high as the moon, there was no way to be seen. Seeing my dismay and fear, the old man said to me:

— Do not be anxious or downcast:
if you would escape from this place,
then eat straightway
what you find around you:
eat the scorpions,
eat the serpents,
yes, eat even
the magic mountain!

> That is the food
> which will give secret nourishment
> and which, in truth,
> is the source of your life.

> — But even if I ate all that,
> there is still the mountain,
> totally blocking our way . . .

> — Have no fear:
> diminish the rest,
> and it, too, will diminish.

Heartened by this advice, I ate what was there, poisonous as it was; and surely enough the rest diminished. At the end of that feast at that lavish table nothing remained. I had levelled the mountain and removed it from our path.

Inside it I saw hundreds and thousands of chasms, full of demons with human faces. From the depths of these gaping abysses, filled with smoke and flames, there rose the sound of human voices. One was saying, 'This well belongs to me!' Another: 'This path is mine!' One said, 'My palace is the holy of holies'. Another cried: 'My garden is a paradise!' One was saying, 'I am the shepherd of this flock'. Another: 'I am the god of all these places'. At length my guide said to me:

> — All these you have seen here
> are bearers of fuel
> to the fires of hell:
> but you, who have mastered yourself,
> have escaped the destruction
> of these infernal reaches.
> The night, meanwhile, is not yet over,
> but soon the light of day will show its face.

Lightheartedly I asked the old man if we had not travelled far enough.

> — Yes! Your words are all too human,
> for the journey through the night
> is not for every weakling.

For the lover, travelling light,
bearing no baggage
but noble poverty,
the night is a protective veil.
In the night you cannot see
the one who seeks;
for the seeker has his own desire,
which serves him as a lamp in darkness;
lovers who light in themselves this lamp
quickly lift the veil of night.

Meanwhile, though the night be dark,
take courage for the dawn is near.

He had hardly spoken these words, when suddenly in
the east I saw the light of dawn. I was overjoyed to regain
my sight; and then I saw a gleaming tower and gateway.
I asked my guide what way it was.

— This is the threshold of that place
where time stands still.
You have left transience behind
and reached salvation.
Go now: you have been released
from this base world.
After so much toil and trial,
rejoice, rejoice!
You have escaped the grievous blade
of Azrael, the angel of death.

And thus it was that we both set foot across the fron-
tier of time.

IV. BEYOND TIME

And so, after passing that last barrier, I suddenly found myself looking at an immense azure expanse. There I saw hundreds of thousands of youths, all of them fresh-faced and happy, but all of them blind. They passed their lives in ignorance of the imperfections of their lowly world and the splendours of superior spheres. To their narrow reason, good coin and bad had the same value.

We passed through this sphere and entered another domain. There I saw circles of listless people, whose souls gave off smoke and whose bodies gave off sparks. They worshipped the self; and their religion was a fireside tale.

The inhabitants of the next stage were extremely numerous. They had two eyes and four idols. They passed their lives in the chains of the four causes of war, and worshipped the four illusions.

I tore myself away from these ignorant people and entered yet another domain of inferior beings, who had gloomy souls and painted faces. They had four eyes and seven idols.

In the next stage I saw a hundred thousand new kings with seven eyes and ten idols. They were all monarchs, and yet all had drunken rogues for friends. They were all judges, and yet all were in prison. Like diamonds, they had the clarity and sparkle of water; but that water was brackish. They were sellers of jewels and yet they were blind. Their appearance was handsome, but their reason was clouded; they were swallowers of poison and sellers of sugar. Not one of them had read the book of God: they had merely glimpsed its title page. Instead of genuine pearls, they threaded false ones; and they boasted, 'Whoever does not find us has lost his way; whoever is not an inhabitant of this city is not a human being'.

The next domain was gleaming with light and brilliant like a mirror. It was inhabited by hundreds and thousands of creatures who were fresh and radiant like houris, but yet lacked both water and fire. At heart they were in harmony with themselves: for themselves both lover and beloved. They each lived in an individual prison, separated from the others. They worshipped light, but that light was of a lowly order. Their eyes were four in number, but they saw with a squint.

The people I met in the next stage were like candles: dark by nature, and yet shining. They had made their noble pedigree their yardstick; and had made of themselves their own nourishment. They had exchanged the sun for the planet Venus, precious gems for glass beads. They each dallied with two mistresses, and each worshipped two idols.

Thus, we who were clear-sighted passed through these regions, and a thousand more like them.

We came to a region where the people were engaged in a thousand forms of prayer. I was enchanted by their beauty, so I asked:

— Who are these creatures?
What do they believe?
What do they pray for?
What do they receive?

— Though they seem fair to you,
those that you see there
are beings of ill omen;
although they seem fortunate,
yet they are wretched:
for all that their nature
partakes of freedom,
still they are captives.

There is a flaw, innate in their creation:
for the very limitation of their vision
has become for them an idol.
What you see here
is an array of religions,
every one of them a prison.

You are with me:
why seek their friendship?
You are in paradise:
why talk of the night?

Open yourself on this road
to more heroic aspirations:
at every moment kindle a fire,
and burn in it all idols
and desire for idols.

Be warned, above all,
that the region ahead of us
has been the undoing
of many a dervish:
How vast it is! How pure its air!
Supreme goal of thousands
of weak-hearted lovers!

The place is heart-ravishing,
soul-ensnaring:
but the people in it
are mere attention mongers.

You have found your companion:
do not slacken your pace;
do not decide to linger here.

You are a child, I tell you;
and the house is full of pretty colours;
and if you don't know it yet,
look at it from afar!

Respectfully I looked and saw a region of pure light.
We set off and made our way to the King and were
dazzled by his splendour.

I gazed on this lord of the heavens, who caused the
creation of the stars of the universe, the source of all
knowledge, wisdom and justice, this king of noble birth
and exquisite speech. He can see everything, without
limitation or doubt; he understands everything but
without the aid of the senses. He is prodigal, but modest;
greedy, but for knowledge. He is one, but he has two
faces: the face of knowledge, turned towards the Father;
and the face of action turned towards the world of forms.
The first face is full of ears to receive the Word; the
second is full of tongues to transmit it.

Thousands of people surrounded him in serried ranks
to receive his truth and glory. All of them were in move-

ment, and yet had neither hands nor feet. All could speak and yet had neither mouths nor tongues. They were beyond mere sensation and imagination. They had permanence, and were beyond 'what' and 'how'. They were orientated towards their true nature and original cause. Among those surrounding him were those leaving for the world of the invisible, and those entering the army of the ineffable. I could see one rank of martyrs, and another of Christian monks and priests. I could see scholars of the divine law, and those who put into practice the outward form of that law. There was one rank of motionless movers, and another of silent speakers. Each one of them said to us:

— Everything here has been prepared for you:
stay, both of you, for the city is yours.

I wanted to rest there a while and acquire wisdom and knowledge; but my guide cried out:

— Did I not warn you
against short-sightedness
and poor discrimination?

The Father is yours, so leave the Son:
Why do you drink from brackish water,
when you can drink from the water of paradise?
Leave this trickle and turn to the ocean:
now that water is there for the taking,
why do you wash your face in the dust?

You are approaching the ultimate stage:
so pay the ferryman his fare,
and leave behind the world of names.
Seek now the visionary Lord of creation.

When he says 'Be', he is the first to be:
he is both essence and outcome of being;
his very intention is a command.

He is shepherd of shepherds
guarding their flocks.
Humbler than the humblest,
his is the throne of majesty.

His is the pen
of the holy book:
he is both essence and substance
of the Qur'an

Embarking on the creative act,
he closed the gates of non-existence.

With him is both the goal of the saints
and their resolve to reach it;
both what the prophets received and what they gave.

Unlike the stars, he has no end:
above him is no movement,
beneath him is no rest;
grounded in joy,
his command is eternal.

And yet, for all his power,
his absolute perfection,
this prime cause of the Word,
silent interpreter of the verb to be,
is the absolute epitome
of all that is gentle, humble and generous.

Veil upon veil conceals his glory;
behind each of them is a world of dervishes:
the highest rank among them
is no more than a little tavern,
its inmates drunk one moment and sober the next,
now engaged in self-affirmation,
now in self-annihilation,
now wrestling with their vices,
now absorbed in contemplation,
performing a thousand labours on their essence,
painters in the workshop of eternity.

So pass by these outhouses,
these little cottages;
up with you! Place your foot
on the whole of creation,
and make your way to the court of the Friend.

Thanks to these words my aspirations were renewed,
and I decided to continue on the way. And that abode,
which I had begun to love, became hateful to me.

V. THE MAN OF LIGHT

And then, suddenly, I ceased to be, and my guide became my 'I'. Thus I was purified of my material origins; from being a child I became a man. With this totally changed nature I continued on my journey.

I walked for years on end around these vast realms, looking at everything. Sometimes I dwelt in the city, sometimes in the desert; sometimes in paradise, sometimes in the depths of hell. Sometimes my heart was a lamp, lighting up the gloomy path of jealousy; sometimes my soul foundered in an ocean of consternation. Sometimes I was brought low by cruel oppression, sometimes intoxicated by the beloved's favour.

When I had finally escaped from all these veils, I arrived in a region where I saw the people walking about saying 'O Lord, increase our confusion yet further!' But this did not happen: knowledge fell effortlessly into their laps. Their view encompassed the human world, and their name extended to the very limits of the world. Since their being had been annihilated in the Supreme Being, they were free of 'why' and 'how', rescued from the clutches of animal bondage, delivered from all ceremonies and necessities of life.

I approached some of those who had reached an even more exalted degree. These beings possessed neither heart, hands, feet nor head. They were totally liberated from the bonds of matter and form, above plurality and contradiction. They had escaped from the wounds and deceptions of fate; and had been relieved from the tedium of fashioning words. They did not see with individual eyes, but as a single body. They were sellers of souls in the hall of nonentity, wearing patched robes in the dervish retreat of eternity. All of them wounded by bolts from beyond; all of them humbled by their own glory.

I saw a light in which someone was moving — as a fish can be seen moving in the waves. This was the effect of the magnificent splendour of their patchwork robes, seen from a distance, as they opened a way before him; and the saints could be seen walking around him — this trailblazer of the rugged path, surrounded by pure hearts on all sides.

In total astonishment I walked the road which led to this place. I no longer had either eyes or heart of my own. I wanted to enter on this Way and belong to this community.

But a lover stepped from out of their ranks, silent, but eloquent. He came up to me, placed his hand on my shoulder and said:

> — You who have flown so high,
> and think to have freed yourself
> from your bonds:
> this place cannot be for you.
> Return to your world
> of prohibitions and permissions:
> you are still tied
> to the world of forms;
> as long as you are sunk
> in the prison of attachment,
> all that is here is beyond your powers:
> you cannot tread the road to that court,
> nor cast your eye on that exalted face.

> The distractions from the Way
> are many in your world:
> when you have passed through it,
> you will taste this kingdom.

> No man by himself
> can know the way forward:
> the Way only shows itself
> to certain people.

> That man of light will be your guide:
> though he seems so close to you,
> he is far-removed indeed.

> He will liberate your thought
> and awaken your creative self.
> Hold to him until you attain
> sincerity and vision:

for he is the guide who brings true friends
through the vision of truth
to the abode of sincerity.
He is the traveller in this world;
he is the one whose eyes are open.

— Who, tell me, is this man of light?

———————————

IV

THE ABODE OF SPRING

Chapter 1

QUOTATIONS FROM SUFI MASTERS

Junaid declares: 'The words of learned sages, firmly grounded in mystical knowledge, are one of the armies of God most high'.

What other power is there,
to fight off the onslaughts
of lust and desire,
than the legions of parables
of those who show the way?

In the Qur'an, it was thus that God called upon his prophet, Mohammed:

'The tales we tell you
concerning the prophets
are the means whereby
we strengthen your heart'.

When, through just desire,
you form an image in your heart,
breathe life into it with the breath
— like a mighty trumpet blast —
of those initiated in the mysteries.
If your heart is shaken
by your restlessness of character,
lend it stability: annotate the story
of those who live by the heart.

Abdullah Ansari gave these last instructions to his companions:

'Memorise a saying by every sage; if you cannot do that, at least memorise his name, so that you may profit from it'.

> You are the one from whose name
> love flows in a stream,
> from whose book and message
> love flows in a stream;
> truly, from your door and roof
> love flows in a stream.

There is a tradition which says that after the resurrection God will say to one of his slaves, bewildered by his own spiritual poverty: 'Did you know such sage and initiate in the mysteries in such and such a place?'

'Yes, I knew him', he will reply. And God will declare: 'I shall forgive you for the love of him'.

> My value, in the succession
> of those who adore you,
> is far too base for me to hope
> for union with you;
> but, inscribed in my heart,
> are the names of the beggars at your gate:
> this is sufficient seal of approval!

Someone asked Mansur al Hallaj, 'What is a disciple?' (murid) He replied, 'He who first and foremost makes the goal of his efforts the court of the divine majesty, and who allows himself no rest and devotes himself to no-one until he has arrived at that goal'.

> For you, I hastened over land and sea,
> crossing deserts and scaling heights;
> from all that was offered
> I turned my face,
> till I gained the sanctuary
> of union with you.

The Sufi Abu Hashim said: 'It is easier to uproot a mountain with a needle than to expel base pride from the heart'.

> Never preen yourself
> that you are prideless:
> for pride is more invisible
> than an ant's footprint
> on a black stone
> in the dark of night.

Dhul-Nun the Egyptian visited a wise man of Maghreb* in order to question him. The sage said to him: 'Why did you come here? If you came to acquire the knowledge of masters ancient and modern, it cannot be done: for all of that is known only to the Creator. If it was in search of the latter that you came, he was there in person at that very spot where you set out'.

> Before, I imagined you
> outside of myself:
> I envisaged you waiting
> at the end of my journey;
> I know, now I've found you,
> it was you I abandoned
> with my very first step.

Ansari, the sage of Herat, declares: 'He travels with whoever looks for him; and having taken the seeker by the hand, he arouses him to go in search of himself'.

Saying of Fudhail ibn Iyad: 'It is through love that I adore God, for I could not bear not to adore him.'

Someone asked a mystic: 'What is an unworthy man?' and he replied: 'Someone who worships God through fear and hope'.

'And how do you worship him?'

'Through perfect love: the sheer love of him keeps me obedient in his service'.

---

*North-West Africa

How could the fervour of your loving victim
vanish in the darkness of the earth?
That flame leaps forth
from his shining soul!
How could he ever take his head
from the collar of faithfulness?
— just like the turtle dove's,
that collar is part of his very neck.

Saying of Maaruf Karkhi: 'The Sufi is in this world as
a guest, and it ill behoves a guest to make demands of his
host; for a well-mannered guest waits, and does not make
demands'.

In the ranks of men of goodwill,
I am your guest, sitting there,
content with all that comes from you;
with my eye cast hopefully on the table of your bounty,
I await your favours, but never demand them.

Someone asked Bayazid: 'What is traditional law and
what is divine law?' He replied: 'Traditional law consists
in retiring from the world; divine law in living with God'.

Shibli fell ill and was taken to hospital. When some
people came to visit him he asked them who they were.
'Your friends,' they replied. Shibli seized a stone and
threatened them with it. At this they all ran away, but
Shibli called them back.
'What presumptuousness! Friends do not flee from
friends, nor do they dodge the stone of their iniquity'.

He is a friend,
who only loves his friend the more,
whatever he suffers at his hand.

It is also recounted of Shibli that once when he was ill
the Caliph sent a Christian doctor to cure him. The
doctor asked him what was his heart's desire.

'That you should become a Muslim', replied Shibli.

'If I became a Muslim, would it cure you, and would you get up from your sick bed?'

'Certainly', replied Shibli. Whereupon he expounded the true faith to the doctor and converted him.

Shibli rose from his bed completely cured; and both men went to the Caliph and told him what had happened.

'I thought I was sending the doctor to the patient', declared the Caliph, 'but really it was the patient I was sending to the doctor'.

Saying of Sahl ibn Abdullah Tustari: 'Whoever wakes up worrying about what he will eat — shun him!'

Abu Said Kharraz said: 'At the beginning of my mystical condition I wanted to guard my "moments".

One day I went into a desert and as I was walking I heard a sound behind me. I didn't allow my heart to pay any attention or my eyes to look; but the sound came nearer and eventually was close behind me. Two great lions climbed on to my shoulders. I did not look at them either as they climbed up or as they got down'.

To him also is attributed the saying, 'Whoever believes he can reach God by his own efforts toils in vain; whoever imagines he can reach God without effort is merely a traveller on the road of intent'.

> By suffering, none attained
> the treasure of mystic union;
> and, strange to say, without suffering,
> none beheld that treasure.
> Of those who ran,
> none captured the onager in the plain;
> yet none took the onager but him who ran.

Saying of Abul-Husain Nuri: 'Him from whom God conceals himself neither guide nor sign will bring to God'.

Saying of Abul-Hassan Qushangi: 'There is nothing worse in the world than a friend whose friendship seeks recompense or has a concealed purpose'.

O sun!
No-one travels the world like you:
tell me something you remember
from your journey;
whom have you seen today
on the path of mystic love,
with dust on his face
and sorrow in his heart?

Someone asked the sage Abu-Said ibn Abil-Khair what Sufism entailed. He replied, 'Whatever you have in mind — forget it; whatever you have in your hand — give it; whatever is to be your fate — face it!'

Saying of Somnun Muhibb: 'The love of the servant for his Lord will not be pure until he senses the shabbiness of the whole world'.

Saying of Abu-Bakr Warraq: 'If you ask Greed who his father is, he will say, "Doubt concerning the decrees of the Almighty". If you ask what his profession is: "Earning degradation and baseness". If you ask what his purpose is: "To be prey to torment and deceit".'

Your daily bread is fixed
from time immemorial:
how long will you waste your energy
on this daily bread?
The profit of your life is in serving God:
so do not transgress the law of devotion.

Saying of Abu-Ali Rudbari: 'No prison confines more
closely than the society of those whose outlook is contrary to one's own'.

For all that the Sufis
call everywhere prison
where the perfume is lacking
that union engenders,
there is no prison narrower
for sigh-laden lovers
than to have to keep company
with unkindred spirits.

The sage Abul-Abbas Qassab saw a dervish stitching a
robe. Every time a stitch displeased him he undid it, to
sew it again.
'This garment is your idol', said the Master.

One day in the presence of the master Abdulkhaliq
Ghujdawani a dervish declared: 'If God most high gave
me the choice between heaven and hell, I would choose
hell, because heaven would be what I desired, whilst hell
would be the will of God'.
The master riposted, 'What use is choice to the
faithful? Wherever he tells us to go, let us go; and
wherever he tells us to stay, let us stay'.

Do nothing
without the assent of the Master,
you who call yourself God's servant:
wherever it is the Master who chooses,
what use is the choice of slaves?'

Someone asked the master Ali Ramitani, 'What is faith?' He replied, 'Uprooting and binding'.

— uprooting one's heart from the world,
to bind it to God.

The master Behauddin Naqshband was asked how far back his genealogy went. He replied: 'Genealogies don't go anywhere'.

Chapter 2

ANECDOTES OF THE WISE

He is held to be wise who, as far as he is able, understands the reality of things, and who has the power to carry out an act in full awareness of all its implications.

A wise old man, who horrified Alexander the Great with his unsightly appearance, said to him:

'Do not begrudge me my ugly exterior,
you who are lacking all virtue and fairness!
This body's a scabbard,
the soul is the sabre:
in the sabre is action
— not in the scabbard'.

Seek the knowledge that is essential;
pay no heed to non-essential knowledge.
And when you have the knowledge you need,
think only of putting it into practice.

Never sit to eat,
Till your stomach is empty;
stand up and leave,
before your stomach is full.

Chosroes, a king of ancient Persia, said: 'I have never regretted what I did not say; but there are many things I have lain in dust and blood for the regret of saying'.

Caesar said: 'I have more power over what I did not say than over what I did say'.

A secret kept
is like an arrow in the hand;
once divulged,
it has left the bow.

O you, who vaunt your reason,
how many times, enslaved by lust,
will you shake your sweetheart's locks
— the chains of madness?

Three men were discussing what was the most distressing affliction.

'Old age and infirmity, coupled with destitution and poverty', said one.

'A sick body, coupled with a host of worries', said another.

'The approach of death, coupled with the absence of good actions', said the third; and on this they were all agreed.

Do not arouse your temper by fasting:
nothing is better than patience and gentleness.
When a fast becomes the cause of trouble,
better to break it than to keep it.

Whoever says 'my table' and 'my bread'
— leave his table and his bread!
Better to eat the greenery in your garden
than that man's roasted lamb!

The only good, for a man of clear sight,
is whatever it is that renders his soul
eternal and blessed.

A king once asked a wise man for advice.

'First', said the sage, 'I shall ask you a question: answer truthfully, which do you prefer — gold, or your enemy?'

'Gold', said the king.

'What you love you will leave behind in this world, and what you hate you will take with you into the next'.

The king wept and said, 'You have given me a counsel which contains all others'.

In a thousand ways
you quarrel with the denizens
of this lowly world,
such is your lust for silver and gold;
silver and gold are your friends,
whoever possesses them, your foe:
you wrest them from his hands
by fraud and violence.
Does reason dictate,
does judgment indicate,
that you should forsake the friend
and carry off the foe?

The wise have said, 'Just as the world prospers thanks to justice, so violence causes its ruin; wherever there is justice, its brilliance extends a thousand leagues; violence casts darkness over a thousand leagues'.

A king said to a dervish, 'Why have I not seen you here for so long?'

'Because I prefer to hear "Why haven't I seen you?" — rather than "Why have you come"?' replied the dervish.

Chapter 3

EXEMPLARY ANECDOTES

Justice without religion is better for the order of the universe than the tyranny of a pious prince.

During the spring festival King Nushirvan of Persia was holding court when he saw one of those taking part conceal a goblet under his arm. The king pretended not to notice and said nothing. When the meeting was over the steward cried out, 'No one is to leave until I have made enquiries: a golden goblet is missing!'

'Let it be!' replied the King. 'Whoever took it will not give it up, and whoever saw him take it will not denounce him'.

Some days later the person in question appeared before Nushirvan dressed in new clothes and wearing new shoes. The king pointed to his clothes, as if to say, 'Does this come from that?' And the man drew back the hem of his garment from his shoes, as if to say, 'This, too, comes from that'. The king smiled and, recognising that the man had been driven by necessity to steal, ordered him to be given a thousand pieces of gold.

When your fault is known to the generous King,
confess it to him and implore his generosity;
never deny your fault,
for that is to commit a second,
worse even than the first.

Caliph Mamun had a page whose job it was to prepare the water for ablutions. Every so often a vase or ewer would disappear. One day Mamun said to the page, 'About those vases and ewers that you keep taking from here — I wish you would sell them back to me!'

'All right', replied the page, 'buy this vase here!'

'How much is it?'

'Two pieces of gold'.

Mamun ordered him to be given the money.

'And will this vase be safe from you now?'

'Certainly', replied the page.

Hajaj, a general and administrator at the time of the Omayyad caliphs, became separated from his body-guards whilst out hunting. He climbed a hill and saw a beduin sitting on the ground picking fleas from his cloak, while his camels grazed all around him. On seeing Hajaj, the camels took fright. The beduin looked up and shouted angrily, 'Who on earth is that, turning up in the desert in such gaudy clothes — God damn him!'

Hajaj did not answer, but moved forward and said, 'Peace be with you, beduin!'

The beduin replied, 'With you be neither the peace, nor the mercy, nor the blessing of God!'

When Hajaj asked him for something to drink he said, 'Get off your horse, and go and drink simply and humbly! By God! I am not your comrade, or your servant!'

Hajaj dismounted and drank some water. Then he said: 'Beduin, who is the best of mortals?'

'The Messenger of God', replied the Beduin, 'God pray for him and save him — and put you to shame!'

'What have you to say', went on Hajaj, 'about Ali ibn Abi-Talib?'

The beduin replied that by virtue of that man's nobility and greatness one dare scarcely pronounce his name.

Hajaj continued: 'And what have you to say about Abdulmalik ibn Marwan?'

The beduin said nothing.

'Answer me!' insisted Hajaj.

'He is an evil man', said the beduin.

'Why?'

'He has committed an error so great that its effects are felt from the east to the west'.

'And what is that?'

'He has given command over the Muslims to that vicious scoundrel Hajaj'.

Hajaj said nothing. Suddenly a bird started up with a cry. The beduin looked at Hajaj and said, 'Who *are* you?'

'Why do you ask?'

The beduin answered, 'That bird just warned me that some soldiers are arriving and that you are their leader'.

He had hardly said this when the bodyguard arrived and saluted Hajaj — whereupon the beduin went pale, and Hajaj ordered him to be taken away.

The next morning, when the table had been laid and Hajaj's friends had gathered, Hajaj called for the beduin.

As he entered, he called out, 'Peace be with you, O prince!'

Hajaj replied: 'I shall not answer you as you answered me. With you be peace likewise! Do you wish to eat?'

The beduin replied, 'This food is yours: if you permit me, I will eat'.

'You have my permission', said Hajaj.

The beduin sat down and, reaching for the food, said, 'In the name of God! If it is God's will, what follows this meal will be favourable!'

Hajaj smiled: 'Don't you remember what happened to me yesterday?'

'God prosper the prince!' said the beduin; 'what happened yesterday between you and me is a secret: do not disclose it now!'

Then Hajaj spoke: 'Beduin, choose one of these alternatives: either place yourself at my disposal and become one of my men; or else I shall send you to Abdulmalik ibn Marwan, telling him what you said about him, so that he may deal with you as he pleases'.

The beduin replied: 'There is yet another possibility'.

'And that is?'

'That is that you should let me return in peace where I belong, and that we should never see each other again'.

Hajaj laughed and ordered him to be given money and sent home.

> When kings take to commerce
> what is there left for merchants to do?

The Commander of the Faithful, Omar,[1] once received a Jew, who complained that the governor of Basra had proved unwilling to settle a debt.

The Caliph asked him, 'Have you a piece of paper?'

'No', replied the Jew.

Omar picked up a potsherd that was lying on the ground and wrote on it: 'Those who complain of you are many; those who speak well of you are few: beware of giving rise to complaints — or else quit the throne of power'. And to close, he added: 'Written by Omar, son of al Khattab'. Now the fear of Omar's rough justice had made such an impression on people's minds, that, when he was presented with the potsherd, the Governor of Basra leapt from his horse and prostrated himself before the still-mounted Jew and paid on the spot all that he owed to him.

> When the lion loses tooth and claw,
> he must suffer the blows of limping foxes.

---

[1] Second Caliph, and organiser of the Muslim conquests.

A young man was caught stealing, and the order was given that his hand should be cut off, according to law. Despite all entreaties from the young man and his mother, the Caliph remained adamant that the law must be fulfilled.

'Cut off his hand', said the Caliph, 'for I will not pardon him his crime: to abstain from punishing him would itself be a crime I could not permit myself'.

'O Caliph', said the mother, 'count that very crime as one of your sins, for which you unceasingly beg God forgiveness and remission'.

These words pleased the Caliph, and he ordered the young man to be freed.

A child of the clan of Hashim was rude to a man of standing. A complaint was made to the boy's uncle, who decided to give him a beating.

'Uncle', said the boy,' 'What I did was done because my reason abandoned me: but you do what you are about to do in full possession of your reason'.

Someone asked Alexander the Great how he had acquired so much power and territory so quickly and so young.

'By winning over my enemies, so that they would curb their disastrous hostility, and uniting with my friends, so that they should be strengthened in the law of friendship'.

Chapter 4

ON GENEROSITY

Who is generous?
— he whose good works are never done
with any gain in view.
Whatever is done for praise, or recompense,
deem it, not generosity, but so much trade.

Someone asked a generous man: 'When you give to the poor, when you are lavish with your gifts to beggars, don't you sense any vanity in your heart of hearts?'

'Away with you!' he retorted. 'My rule is to apply myself to giving; like the strainer in the hand of the cook: everything the cook pours in passes through the strainer; but the strainer does not thereby lay any claim to the merit of giving'.

A mystic, describing another such, said, with regard to his wisdom and knowledge, 'He is like someone who sets the table, not someone who owns it: he regards himself as being on a par with his fellow guests — or even less: a mere hanger-on'.

When, in the great reception hall,
the master decks his table for the poor,
he is but a child on the path,
if he does not realise
that he it is, not they,
who is the sponger.

Whoever, rather than feeding
the dog of his own appetites,
feeds a few morsels
of bread to a dog,
deserves that his masters
. avow themselves his slaves.

In Medina there lived an industrious scholar who was
accomplished in all the religious sciences. One day he
happened to be walking near the slave market, when he
saw a young girl singer, whose voice was the envy of the
planet Venus and whose looks disconcerted the very sun.
He fell in love with her perfection, and was enraptured
by the locks of her hair and the mole on her cheek.
Listening to her singing, he was transported from being
into non-being; he left the narrow path of wisdom to
follow the broad road leading to the palace of bewilder-
ment.

Even singly,
fair face and fair voice
can ravish the heart;
when they are united,
the wisest of men is perturbed.

He threw off the robe of wisdom and dressed in the
homespun of dishonour. Casting shame aside, he
wandered through the bazaar district of Medina. His
friends began to reproach him, but to no avail. He expressed his state in these words:

'How could a lover,
seeing her radiance,
sidestep disaster?
To my ears, all your blame
is a puff of wind, fanning the flame'.

This story reached the ears of Abdullah, son of Jafar.
He bought the slave for forty thousand pieces of gold and
ordered her to sing in the way that had so captivated the
scholar. Then he asked her who had taught her to sing

like that. Such and such a singer, she said. And Abdullah had her brought to him as well.

Then he called for the scholar and asked him, 'Do you want to hear that song which makes you lose your mind — sung by the woman who taught the young girl?'

'Yes', he replied.

On hearing the song, the scholar was beside himself and fell down unconscious, so that everyone thought he was dead. Abdullah cried, 'See quickly if we have committed the crime of killing that man!'

But when water was thrown over his face, the scholar came to his senses.

'I did not realize', said Abdullah, 'that your love for that girl had reached such a degree'.

'By God', he replied, 'what is hidden in my heart far surpasses what has manifested itself'.

'And now, do you want to hear that song sung by the young girl?' asked Abdullah.

'You saw what happened when I heard it sung by another, whom I do not love: what will happen if I hear it from the lips of my beloved?'

'If you see her', asked Abdullah, 'will you recognize her?'

'You ask me will I know her, who has robbed me of heart and faith! By God, in all the world she is all that I do know!'

Then Abdullah said: 'She is yours; I swear I have not so much as looked at her'.

Ibrahim ibn Sulaiman ibn Abdulmalik ibn Marwan tells the following story:

At the time of the upheavals which led to the passing of the Caliphate from the Omayyads to the Abbasids, while the Abbasids were arresting the Omayyads and putting them to death, I had stationed myself outside Kufa on the terrace of a palace which overlooked the plain. On seeing some black banners coming out of Kufa, it occurred to me that it was a troop of soldiers in search of me. I came down from the terrace, and, wearing a disguise, went into the city. Now I did not know anyone in whose house I could hide. I arrived at the gates of a palace and went inside. There I saw a horseman, of handsome bearing, surrounded by a group of pages and servants.

When I saluted him he said, 'Who are you, and what do you want?'

'I am a fugitive, in fear of my enemies', I said, 'and so I took refuge here'.

He took me in and gave me a room next to the women's quarters. There I stayed for several days, in the best of circumstances: my every wish was catered for — food, drink, clothing — without any questions being asked. Every day my host mounted his horse, rode off, and later returned.

One day I said to him: 'Every day I see you ride off and then return: what is your errand?'

He replied, 'Ibrahim ibn Sulaiman has killed my father. Rumour has it that he is hiding in this town. Every day I go out in the hope that perhaps I shall find him and avenge the death of my father'.

On hearing this I was aghast at my own ill fortune: I had been cast by destiny into the house of someone who wished my death. I felt tired of existence. I asked him his name, and his father's name, and realized that what he said was true.

Then I said to him: 'Noble sir, in granting me protection, you have acquired many rights over me. And so I have the duty to point out your enemy to you — and thus curtail all your comings and goings. I am Ibrahim ibn Sulaiman: take vengeance on me for the blood of your father!'

He did not believe me: 'I suppose life is weighing you down, and that you wish to be freed of this torment?'

'No, by God! It was I who killed your father', I replied; and I told him all the details.

Then he realized that I was telling the truth. His cheeks flushed and his eyes became bloodshot. Then he said: 'You will not be long in joining my father; and it will be he who has vengeance on you. But as for myself: I have granted you protection and I will not cheat you of it. Get up and go; for I am not sure of myself; and God forbid that I should do you any harm'.

Then he gave me a thousand pieces of gold, which I took and fled.

Chapter 5

ON LOVE

Two sages had taken up the topic of love.

One declared: 'The hallmarks of love are misfortune and suffering. Incessantly the lover experiences torment and affliction'.

The other replied, 'Enough! I suppose you have never seen peace follow war, or tasted the delight of union after separation! None in the world are more delightful than those who, with a pure heart, give themselves to love; and none cruder than those insensitive beings who remain aloof from such cares!'

> The light of the One
> who is loved with love
> is the beauty of the human heart.
> How could he aspire to beauty,
> whose own heart is not beautiful?
> — What argument in proof of this?
> — that like inclines to like,
> that is my argument!

A famous beauty began to lose her looks, and her former admirers no longer sought her company. I said to one of them:

'After all, she is the same person as before ... How can you desert her?'

'Have a care what you say', he replied. 'That which enraptured my heart and captivated my reason was a spirit which breathed in the harmonious form of her limbs, the litheness of her body, the fineness of her skin, the delicacy of her voice. Now that this spirit has left them, how should I love those dead forms?'

> The rose has fled the garden;
> what shall I do
> with thorns and dried grass?
> The bird has flown;
> what shall I do with the cage?

Chapter 6

ON HUMOUR

The Prophet Mohammed is quoted as saying, 'The believer is high-spirited and speaks pleasantly; the hypocrite is sullen and frowning'.

The Prophet once told an old woman that the likes of her would never enter paradise. The old woman burst into tears. Then Mohammed added: 'No, almighty God will first give them back their youth, and raise them up more beautiful than they ever were — and *then* he will lead them into paradise!'

A blind man was making his way one dark night with a lamp in his hand and a jar on his shoulder. Someone came and rudely said to him, 'Fool! For you, night and day are one; for your eyes, darkness and light are the same! So what is the use of that lamp?'
The blind man smiled and answered, 'This lamp is not for me, but for sightless scatterbrains like yourself: so that they don't bump into me and break my jar'.

Constantly you prostrate yourself:
— not in order to worship,
but to lay on the ground
the mighty burden of your nose!

213

Bahlul one day entered the court of Harun al Rashid. A minister said to him, 'Good news, Bahlul! The Commander of the Faithful has appointed you to be in charge of pigs and monkeys'.

'Very well', said Bahlul, 'listen to me and carry out my orders'.

Someone asked Mulla Nasrudin who was the older — himself or his brother.

'I am the older', he replied, 'but give him a year, and he'll be the same age as me'.

A man was trying to sue a clown for ten pieces of silver. The judge asked him if he could produce a witness, and he replied that he could not. When the judge spoke of administering the oath to the clown, the other replied, 'What consideration does he deserve? He makes promises as blithely as the Arabs drink curdled milk!'

'Your honour', said the clown, 'at the mosque we have an Imam who is chaste, truthful and upright: why don't your administer the oath to him instead — and put this man out of his misery!'

Someone asked a child if he would like his father to die, so as to gain his legacy.

'No', he replied, 'I would like someone to kill him: that way I'd not only get his legacy but the blood-money as well'.

A scholar declared from his pulpit: 'When the mysterious palace of the other world becomes visible, God will pardon the white beards their faults for the sake of the black beards; and, conversely, on the day of judgment the black beards will be under the protection of the white beards'.

On hearing this, a little man with a red beard passed his hand over his chin and said, 'I don't figure in this account, so I am of no use in this world or the next!'

A beautiful slave was walking along and a man began to tail after her. Finally she asked him, 'Do you want to do what my master does with me?'

'Yes, indeed!' he replied.

'Well', she said, 'here comes my master: you can do with him what he does with me'.

Chapter 7

FROM OTHER POETS

Imad-uddin, the Faqih of Kirman, was the sheikh of a dervish retreat. He used to read his verses to whoever visited the *khanaqa*, and would ask them to suggest improvements. And so it is said that his verses were composed by all the inhabitants of Kirman.

Rudaki

> Time has given me
> this liberating counsel —
> and time, when you consider,
> consists entirely of good advice:
> beware of envying
> the happy days of others:
> how many people
> will envy you yours!

Daqiqi

> I have lingered too long,
> and become contemptible
> — as the water in a pond
> becomes putrid through tranquility.

Farrukhi

> From many a worthy person,
> time and again, in every town,
> I have heard tell
> of a river of paradise,
> and eight heavens:
> well, I have seen a thousand paradises,
> a thousand heavenly rivers, and more;
> but what use is that to me,
> when I have to return here,
> my lips parched with thirst?
> To contemplate with the eye
> treasures the hand cannot buy
> is like a severed head
> in a basin of gold.

Rashiddudin Wathvath

> My eye is full of the forms of my beloved:
> I cannot tell my eye from my beloved.
> Either she has taken the place of my eye,
> or my eye has become — my beloved.

Souzani

> I am a thousand times more evil
> than anything you know of evil:
> in this no one knows me
> as I know myself.
> Outwardly I am evil,
> but inwardly I am even more so.
> God and I, we know
> my exterior and my interior.
> Satan may be my guide
> in the occasional venial sin;
> but in a hundred deadly sins
> I show Satan the way.

Khaqani

Cease, O Khaqani, to let yourself
be swept off your feet by beautiful women!
In reality their apparent form is a mirror,
whose outward face is brilliant,
but whose inner is nothing but darkness.

Jurjani

I do not care for the golden bowl
in which my enemy will contemplate my blood.

The narcissus flower:
sweet to look at, bitter to taste.

Khayali

The heart of your lovers
is the target of the trouble you cause:
a whole people busies itself with you
— you who keep yourself from view.

Chapter 8

FABLES

A poisonous scorpion decided to go on a journey. When it arrived at a large stretch of water it stood rooted to the spot, daring neither to advance nor to turn back. Seeing this, a turtle took pity on it and bade it climb on to its back.

As the turtle was swimming for the opposite shore a strange sound reached its ears.

'What is that noise?' it asked.

'That', said the scorpion, 'is my sting, which I am striking against your shell. Even though I know that it doesn't have any effect, I simply can't help doing it — it's my nature'.

The turtle thought to itself: 'The best thing to do is to deliver this malicious creature from its frightful nature and to protect creatures of good will from the evil it might cause'. So saying, it dived, and the scorpion was swallowed by the waves — so that it might as well never have existed.

A camel and a donkey were journeying together. They arrived at the bank of a broad river, and the camel went in first.

'Come on!' it shouted, 'The water is only belly-high'.

'That's right', said the donkey. 'But there are bellies and bellies'.

A peacock and a crow met on a lawn and examined their respective merits and defects.

Said the peacock to the crow, 'Those red boots that you have would go very well with my satin shot with gold and my illuminated brocade. No doubt when we came from the dark night of non-existence into the dazzling daylight of existence, we must have put on the wrong footwear'.

'Not a bit of it', said the crow. 'Your robe matches my boots perfectly: evidently in that sleep of confusion you put on my robe and I put on yours'.

A burden that heaven and earth
refuse to carry
can hardly be borne
by mere bodily force:
strengthen your thought
with the aid of those
who follow the path of love;
for it is by your spiritual strength
that you will be able to carry that burden.

On the day of combat,
the blow comes from the lance:
pretensions come from man.

Epilogue

I hope of the noble character of my readers, that if they find a fault in my work, they will cover it with the hem of the robe of pardon and indulgence, and not strive to divulge it with the tongue of denigration and malice.

Jami, 892 A.H.
1487 A.D

THE SUFIS

The Sufis is the pivotal work which heralded the revelation of the astonishing richness and variety of the Sufi thought system and its contribution to human culture contained in Idries Shah's many books on the subject.

Today, studies in Sufism, notably through Shah's research and publication, are pursued in centres of higher learning throughout the world, in the fields of psychology, sociology, and many other areas of current human concern.

'For the vital and concentrated knowledge contained in his writings, the work of Idries Shah must be considered a major cultural and psychological event of our time.' – **Psychology Today**

'Must be the biggest society of sensible men there has ever been on earth'.

Ted Hughes: *The Listener*

THE SUFIS
by Idries Shah

The Octagon Press

THE RELIGION OF THE SUFIS

Constantly quoted and widely read for the three centuries since it was written, this book by a scholar of the East based in India gives an excellent insight into what the Sufis of the time gave out as their teaching, and what scholars and others thought of them. It well vindicates its prefatory phrase: 'containing what has been reported by those who know what is manifest, and see what is concealed; as well as by those who are attached to exterior forms, and by those who discern the inward meaning . . . without hatred, enmity and scorn, and without taking a part for the one, or against the other side of the question.'

'*The Dabistan* contains more recondite learning, more entertaining history, more beautiful specimens of poetry, more ingenuity and wit . . . than I ever saw collected in a single volume' — *Sir William Jones*

'A work by an Oriental and written for Orientals, but we of the West may equally profit by its contents'
— *Professor A. V. Williams Jackson*, Professor of Indo-Iranian Languages in Columbia University.

THE RELIGION OF THE SUFIS
Translated from 'The Dabistan' by David Shea and Anthony Troyer
Introduction by Idries Shah

The Octagon Press

TEACHINGS OF HAFIZ

Hafiz of Shiraz is unquestionably in the front rank of world classical poets. As a lyricist and Sufi master, his work is celebrated from India to Central Asia and the Near East as are Shakespeare, Dante or Milton in the West: Goethe himself, among many other Westerners, was among the master's admirers.

This collection is by the eminent linguist and explorer Gertrude Bell who (as Dr. A. J. Arberry says) 'early in her adventurous life conceived an enthusiasm for Hafiz which compelled her to write a volume of very fine translations'.

TEACHINGS OF HAFIZ
Translated by Gertrude Lowthian Bell
Introduction by Idries Shah

The Octagon Press

LEARNING HOW TO LEARN

Condensed from over three million words, these conversations involve housewives and cabinet ministers, professors and assembly line workers, on the subject of how traditional psychology can illuminate current human, social and spiritual problems. More than a hundred tales and extracts from Sufi lore, ranging from the 8th Century Hasan of Basra to today's Ustad Khalilullah Khalili, are woven into Shah's narratives of how and why the Sufis learn, what they learn and how spiritual understanding develops and deteriorates in all societies.

'A remarkable tour de force based on the author's long experience teaching many kinds of pupils . . . provides invaluable guidance to the kind of instruction which is alone worth having . . . Full of wit, wisdom and common sense' — *Asian Affairs* (Journal of the Royal Society for Asian Affairs).

'packed with important information' — *New Society*

'This long-awaited book is regarded as a key to Shah's corpus of 25 volumes which have had considerable effect upon psychology, sociology and anthropology throughout the world . . . Astonishing in its pioneer content and treatment of human problems'
— *Newsletter, World Future Studies Federation.*

'A watershed in studies of the mind' — *Psychology Today (Choice of the Month)*

LEARNING HOW TO LEARN
Idries Shah
The Octagon Press

THE WORLD OF THE SUFI

Many of the great scientists of the Middle Ages wrote Sufi books: but what had these 'ecstatic mystics' to do with optics, historiography, psychology and theories of evolution? Many of them were executed, exiled and imprisoned for blasphemy, dangerous innovations and believing in ancient philosophies: nowadays almost as many — the same ones — are revered as saints of Islam. But if they were saints of Islam, why did the Christian apologists, including St. Thomas Aquinas, The Blessed Ramon Lull and Dante appropriate so much of their work? *The World of the Sufi* is a collection of studies of Sufis and Dervishes of today and yesterday: their exercises and ideas, their influences on religion, science and psychology: from classical master to the present day.

THE WORLD OF THE SUFI
Introduction by Idries Shah

The Octagon Press

A FOOL OF GOD: MYSTICAL VERSE OF BABA TAHIR

One of the earliest Persian Sufi poets, Baba Tahir is famous for his use of rustic dialect rather than polished style. In his mystical love-poetry are seen close analogies with Western mystical writings. He is one of the four great pioneers of the quatrain (the others were Abu Said, Ansari and Omar Khayyam) and his songs are still widely sung and revered in Central Asia. Known as 'The Naked' because of his disdain for outward show, Tahir was visited by Sultan Tughrul Beg and, it is believed, granted him victory over his enemies, providing that he always upheld justice. Perhaps for this reason, the recitation of his work is believed by some to grant the heart's desire of an honest man or woman.

A FOOL OF GOD: MYSTICAL VERSE OF BABA TAHIR
Persian text with a translation by Edward Heron-Allen

The Octagon Press